MILLER'S
SILVER
& PLATE
Antiques Checklist

Consultant: John Wilson

General editors:
Judith and Martin Miller

MILLER'S

MILLER'S ANTIQUES CHECKLIST: SILVER AND PLATE

Consultant: John Wilson

First published in Great Britain in 1994 by Miller's
an imprint of Reed Consumer Books Limited
Michelin House
81 Fulham Road
London
SW3 6RB
and Auckland, Melbourne, Singapore and Toronto

Series Editor	Alison Starling
Editor	Alison Macfarlane
Art Editor	Geoff Fennell
Illustrator	Simon Miller
Special Photography	Ian Booth
Production	Heather O'Connell
Index	Hilary Bird

A CIP catalogue record for this book is available from the
British Library

ISBN 1 85732 272 X

Set in Caslon 540, Caslon 224 bold and Caslon 3
Origination and printing by Madarin Offset
Printed in Malaysia

Cover picture: *An octagonal pepper caster; Charles Adam; 1718*
Picture on p.1: *A George III oval soup tureen and cover, Thomas Robins,
1810*

A table candlestick, Robert Sharp, London, 1805

CONTENTS

WINE

SHEFFIELD PLATE

AMERICAN SILVER

MISCELLANEOUS

HOW TO USE THIS BOOK

When I first started collecting antiques although there were many informative books on the subject I still felt hesitant when it came to actually buying an antique. What I really wanted to do was interrogate the piece – to find out what it was and whether it was genuine.

The *Silver* Checklist will show you how to assess a piece as an expert would, and provides checklists of questions you should ask before making a purchase. The answer to most (if not all) of the questions should be "yes", but remember there are always exceptions to the rule: if in doubt, seek expert guidance.

The book is divided into collecting categories, including candlesticks, decorative tableware and wine. It has separate sections on American silver and Sheffield plate and electroplate, and a miscellaneous section of inexpensive collectables. At the back of the book is a glossary, bibliography and a list of makers and their marks.

Treat the book as a knowledgeable companion, and soon you will find that antique collecting is a matter of experience, and of knowing how to ask the right questions.

JUDITH MILLER

Each double-page spread looks at items belonging to a particular category of collecting.

The first page shows a carefully-chosen representative item of a type that can usually be found at antiques stores or auction houses (rather than only in museums).

The caption gives the date and dimensions of the piece shown, and a code for the price range of this type of article.

A checklist of questions gives you the key to recognizing, dating and authenticating antique pieces of the type shown.

Useful background information is provided about the craftsman, factory or type of ware.

PEPPER CASTER

Pepper caster by Samuel Wood; 1761; ht 6in (15cm); value code B

Identification checklist for a mid-18thC pepper caster
1. Is the caster marked under the base in a ...
2. Are there also marks on the cover?
3. Has the piercing remained intact?
4. Is the finial in good, unrestored condition?
5. If there is a coat-of-arms, is it contemporary with the date of the caster?
6. Does the join between foot and body seem ...
7. Is it a tall bulbous shape?

Pepper casters
Casters were made from the late 17thC, frequently in sets of three, with one big and two smaller casters. The larger caster was used for sugar; smaller ones were for pepper. Small casters which have a design engraved on the cover but are not pierced are occasionally seen – these were for dry mustard. Mustard was not castable so the lid would have to have been removed to serve the contents. Casters diminished in popularity towards the end of the 18thC, when they were replaced by cruets (see pp.52-3). Single

casters are not un... sets command a ... ones are often si...
The caster in ... was made in 176... Wood, one of the ... most prolific cast... time. This tall ba... remained basicall... throughout the c... the foot became ... taller. The caster ... tant features whi... desirability:
* highly decorati... engraving on the ...
* a contemporary ...

Marks, signatures
and serial numbers
are explained.

The second page
shows you what
details to look for.

Information helps
you to detect fakes,
copies and
reproductions.

Marks
Marks should be found on both
the body and the cover. The
body tends to be marked under
the base in a group, although
early ones and those from the late
18thC are sometimes marked in a
straight line on the body. The
cover is usually marked with a
lion passant and possibly a
maker's mark. Covers with no
marks should give cause for
suspicion.

Charles Adam, a well-known
maker, would be highly sought
after and, in perfect condition,
worth about 50% more than a circular one. The top now has a
bezel (trim) and this will probably
be marked.

Further photographs
show:
* items in a similar
style by the same
craftsman or factory
* similar, but perhaps
less valuable wares
that may be mistaken
for the more
collectable type
* common variations
on the piece shown in
the main picture
* similar wares by
other craftsmen
* the range of shapes
or decorative motifs
associated with a
particular factory or
period.

The lighthouse-shaped caster
became popular in the early
18thC. The cover is attached to
the base by a bayonet fitting,
where two locking lugs are slotted into a flange and rotated to
secure the two pieces. This caster
was made by John Smith in 1703.
Such early casters tend to be
quite heavy and solid in appearance because pepper was expensive and merited a good holder.
This one is worth nearly ten
times more than the one in the
main picture.

Irish provincial silver is avidly
collected, not only in Ireland, but
also on the international market,
and this robust kitchen pepper,
made by William Clark of Cork,
would be highly sought after.
Casters of this type are termed
kitchen peppers because they
have a handle to enable the cook
more easily to season the food.
Peppers of this distinctive shape
date from before c.1730 and are
relatively scarce. This one is fairly simple in form, some have
more decoratively pierced covers.

Because octagonal shaped casters
are highly decorative, usually
early and rarer than circular ones
they always command a premium. This 1718 caster made by

Bun peppers, so-called because of
their plump form, were produced
throughout the 18thC; this one
was made in 1731 by John
Gamon, a prolific maker. Bun
peppers are smaller than most
others, measuring around
3in/7.5cm and were among the
least expensive casters.
* Bun peppers are usually
marked in the piercing. As there
is no bezel on the cover, the tops
fall off easily, and many were lost
and replaced. If the cover is not
contemporary with the base the
pepper is best avoided.

57

Hints and tips help
you to assess factors
that affect value – for
example, condition
and availability.

7

INTRODUCTION

In Great Britain domestic silver has survived in great quantities from the late 17thC onwards. Ready supplies of the metal coupled with skilled craftsmen and wealthy purchasers combined to produce a legacy which has managed to pass the ravages of war and civil strife virtually unscathed. In the United States the earliest piece of silver dates to c.1651, and any silver from before the middle of the 18thC is very rare. It was not really until the 19thC that the Americans developed their own highly decorative style which is very collectable today.

English silver has from very early times been stamped with official marks guaranteeing the purity of the metal, and as a by-product this system has provided a record of the date, place of origin and the maker. Originally the piece was made by the person whose maker's mark was struck on the object, but by the third quarter of the 18thC, when workshop production became popular, this was no longer the case. Frequently other silversmiths in the factory would make the objects which would then be stamped with the name of the maker whose workshop it was. In the United States there was never a central marking system, and most silver is only stamped with the name or initials of the silversmith, making it difficult to date any pieces accurately.

Most silver enthusiasts collect silver according to a style that appeals to them. This can be anything from the very plain pieces made at the beginning of the 18thC, to rococo examples produced 50 years later, and neo-classical pieces later on in the century. Increasing wealth and new mass production techniques in the 19thC made silver more readily available, and as a result a greater range of objects and a broader range of quality ensued. However, 19thC silver was held in little esteem until the combined pioneering efforts of some leading auction houses and a number of dealers brought it the attention it deserved from buyers. At the upper end of the market is the output of Rundell, Bridge and Rundell, who produced excellent-quality pieces, including many display items; at the other extreme is the variety of inexpensive small wares made to suit new fashions and lower incomes. Victorian inventiveness began to fail towards the end of the 19thC, and much 20thC silver consists of reproductions of earlier styles – these tend to be of second-hand value and are not particularly collectable. Exceptions include a number of Art Nouveau and Art Deco items, and some highly individual pieces made by craftsmen such as Gilbert Marks, Omar Ramsden and their present-day equivalents.

A private buyer can find out most of the information he needs to know about silver from museums. He then has two major sources of supply – private dealers and sale rooms – both of which can provide practical help. Most specialist dealers are enthusiasts themselves and will be more than happy to talk about their wares, but remember they may not take kindly to you using their stock as museum exhibits. If buying at a sale always ask for a condition report on the lot you are interested in, and read the catalogue description carefully. Make sure prices are realistic. The value of a piece of silver depends greatly on a good surface colour, original condition and a lack of repair, and as this is not easy to see in artificial light try to view a piece in daylight. If buying at auction, do not go above your set price limit; buyers who think "just one more bid should get it" often end up paying anything from 20 to 30 per cent more than they anticipated! The major attraction of the sale room to collectors, particularly those just starting off, is that the goods can be freely handled – nothing learnt from a book is a substitute for physically handling an article. The best advice for a buyer at auction is to view an item carefully, note any good or bad points, attend the sale and then compare the price paid with your own ideas. In time you will gain enough confidence to ignore the estimates, negotiate with dealers on a basis of knowledge and pounce on that rarity – an unrecognized bargain.

Buy only what appeals to you personally – there are many attractive domestic items capable of giving pleasure for hundreds, rather than thousands, of pounds. However, if you are buying for investment, remember items that are inexpensive at present may well fetch low prices when you try to re-sell. Avoid items that are in poor condition and be careful not to buy singles of things which are usually made in pairs.

Collections are more interesting if they have a theme – this may be a single maker, a family or workshop, or even a particular type of object or period. There is, for example, an astonishing variety of mustard pots, ranging from the conventional to the bizarre – whatever you decide upon, there are societies to cater for specialist and general collectors.

Once you have got your piece of silver home it is important to look after it. The first thing to do is clean it thoroughly – if you have done your homework properly you should not find any unpleasant surprises at this stage! Any proprietary cleaner removes a little of the surface so silver should be cleaned as little as possible. Use a long term cleaner or, particularly for intricate items, one of the preparations which foams and can be applied with a sponge. Protect the marks with your thumb, and use a cloth or chamois leather specially kept for silver to avoid scratching. Particularly intricate pieces need to be dipped – ensure that the silver is well-rinsed otherwise the smell of the cleaning solution will linger for days. Display items can be protected professionally against tarnish at a relatively modest cost, provided that they are not handled on a regular basis.

Finally, be aware of what you have got. Keep useful records such as catalogues and invoices. Photograph pieces or make a video recording, and keep insurance lists and prices up to date. Having to deal with an insurer with inadequate descriptions is a frustrating business and you owe it to yourself to look after your property to the best of your ability.

JOHN WILSON

BASICS

HALLMARKS
The Goldsmith's Hall in London still strikes silver with hallmarks today. Most English silver has four marks, which, historically, guaranteed that a piece of silver was of the required legal standard. Although hallmarks are a good guide to age and authenticity they should not be regarded as definitive as they can be worn to illegibility, faked, or even let-in from other pieces of metal.

Sterling silver
Sterling is the British term for silver that is at least 92.5% pure. From 1300 the mark was a leopard's head, by 1478 it had a crown. In 1544 it was a lion passant walking to the left, and from 1820 the lion was uncrowned.

Britannia standard
This was a higher standard of silver required between 1697 and 1720. On this standard of silver the town and sterling marks were replaced by Britannia and a lion's head in profile.

*The original sterling marks were revived in 1720, but the Britannia mark was sometimes used after that date as an alternative to indicate silver of the higher quality.
*The initials used by makers with the Britannia standard are the first two letters of of the surname; with sterling silver it is the initials of the Christian name and surname.

The town mark
This varied according to the assay office of the individual town (see pp.180-181). Sometimes the London mark of a leopard's head was used on provincial silver in addition to the town mark.

The date letter
This appears in London from 1478 and later in other parts of the country. It is unique from year to year and assay office to office, but usually follows an alphabetical sequence. The letter is always enclosed by a shield.

The maker's mark
Used on silver from 1363, the early marks were signs or symbols, as few people could read; this remained the case until the late 17thC when initials and symbols were combined, the symbols falling from use during the next 100 years.

The sovereign's head
Used between 1784 and 1890 (and in Dublin from 1807) to indicate that duty has been paid on the item. The mark for George III after 1785 is hard to distinguish from those used for George IV and William IV.

Forged marks
Marks are struck with steel dies, but most forged marks are struck with brass dies, known as "soft punches" because of the lack of clarity in the resultant image. Marks can also be cast from a genuine piece. If this has happened there tends to be small granulations visible in the outline of the stamping which would not be there if the marks were struck.

Transposed marks
These are sets of marks taken from damaged or low-value objects and inserted into more saleable pieces. They can be detected by discrepancies between the style and date indicated by the hallmark, and the presence of a faint outline around the marks where they have been soldered on to a piece (which can be seen by breathing on to the area).

Duty dodgers
By not sending silver for assay the silversmith avoided the duty. There are two types of duty dodging. The first occurred when the silversmith made a small piece of silver such as a dish, sent it for assay, and then cut out the marks and transferred them to a larger piece. The second type occurred when the silversmith cut out the marks from another, usually older, small piece of silver that had been properly hallmarked, and set them into the base of a

larger, heavier piece, adding his own maker's mark and sometimes striking it again over the date letter to disguise it. These can be detected where the maker's mark is of a more recent date than the hallmark. Although they do not conform to the Hallmarking Acts, these items are at least made by the man whose mark appears on them.

Illegal alterations

In 1844 it was an offence to make unhallmarked additions to a piece or to alter its purpose, and today it is illegal to sell such alterations. These are the best-intentioned fakes as the purpose was simply to make more useful or fashionable an otherwise unwanted item.

DECORATION

Surfaces of silver are rarely plain (except for early 18thC English silver and much 18thC American silver). The main types of decorations are:

Engraving

This involves cutting out a pattern in the silver with a sharp tool. For arms, inscriptions and other marks of ownership the work was done by hand. The decoration cannot be seen on the reverse. Fine engraving was carried out in Europe, particularly in the Netherlands and Germany. Some of the finest British engravers were William Hogarth, Simon Gribelin and James Sympson. American engraving is rare, but some good examples were produced by Nathaniel Hurd and Joseph Leddel. Unlike British engravers, many American engravers signed their work.

A George II silver salver engraved with stylized flower-filled urns, masks, classical portrait medallions and crests.

Bright-cutting

This was popular at the end of the 18thC. It employs the same methods as engraving, but uses a burnished steel tool to cut the metal which polishes the silver as it cuts to produce a sharp design which reflects the light.

A 1780 silver salver with bright-cut engraving.

Chinoiserie

Chinoiserie flat chasing, popular in the late 17thC, incorporates scenes of oriental figures, birds and exotic landscapes into the design. The charmingly naive subjects are generally very similar and it has been suggested that a single specialist chaser was responsible for all the pieces. Any items of silver chased with Chinoiserie decoration are highly collectable and command exceptionally high prices.

A Charles II casket, London, 1683, decorated with Chinoiserie scenes.

Chasing

Chasing appears on silver in the middle of the 17thC and again in the middle of the 18thC. It is a form of relief decoration where the metal is pushed into the required pattern with a hammer or punch, and unlike engraving no silver is removed. The pattern is raised clearly above the surface and the imprint can be seen on

11

the reverse. Common motifs include flowers, foliage and scrolls of various types.
*Victorians often decorated earlier silver with chasing.
*High-quality chasing was produced by Paul de Lamerie and Aymé Videau in the 18thC.
*It is sometimes difficult to differentiate between 18thC and 19thC chasing, but genuine 18thC work tends to be more natural and lively compared to the slightly mechanical feel of Victorian work.
*Silver chased in the 18thC was marked after it was decorated. When chasing has been added at a later date it will go through the marks – chasing which has been applied first will have the marks superimposed over it.

A William III silver chocolate pot, William Lukin, London, 1701, with cut-card decoration.

Borders
Border styles can provide some indication to the date that a piece of silver was made. However, it is important to realise that many 18thC borders were repeated in the 19thC.

A fine George II cup and cover c.1740, finely chased with a band of foliage, scrolls and Bacchic masks.

Flat chasing
This is the same as chasing, but the decoration appears in low relief. It can be distinguished from engraving as it bears the reverse pattern on the inside.

Cut-card decoration
Good-quality late 17th and early 18thC pieces of silver are sometimes overlaid with cut-card decoration – pieces of silver, usually in the form of foliage, which are made separately and then soldered to the body to provide attractive reinforcement for the handle sockets or spouts of coffee pots and similar items.
Sometimes cut-card decoration is applied beneath the central foot of salvers, in which case it is not visible. Such decoration is a true sign of quality.

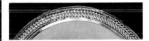

Gadroon borders were popular on early silver from c.1690 to 1700. This example taken from a later 17thC piece of silver is typical. The border is stamped and therefore fragile and prone to splitting.

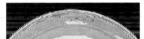

Simple moulded borders such as this were applied to wares at the turn of the 18thC.

The moulded border was replaced by a simple shell and scroll border in the 1730s.

A later development of the border above is this one from 1758 which is similar but more pronounced. This type of border was also repeated in the Victorian times when it tended to be slightly more elaborate.

By the end of the 18thC borders had become plainer. Those dating from 1780 were beaded.

Borders from the 1790s and 1800 are either reeded as illustrated by this example, or threaded.

By the time of the Regency period borders had become very fancy and elaborate.
*Cartouches around coats-of-arms are often similarly intricate and decorative.

This leafy shell and gadroon Regency border is more typical than the one above and features on a wide number of salvers, plates, entrée dishes and other silver wares.

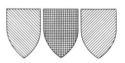

An alternative to the 1790s' reeded border above is this bright-cut example.

Coats-of-arms

It has always been fashionable for families to engrave their coat-of-arms, crest or monogram within a decorative cartouche in a prominent place on a piece of silver, especially on larger items. The type of shield and style of cartouche can provide help in dating a piece that lacks a full set of marks, and sometimes it is even possible to trace the arms to a particular individual.

Top Earl, centre left Duke, centre right Marquess, bottom left Viscount, bottom right Baron.

On some larger pieces a full set of armorials can appear. This is a coat-of-arms surrounded by a cartouche, mantling, a motto, and for members of the peerage, a coronet and supporters. Arms are always described from behind. Although the husband's arms always appear on the left as one is looking at them, they are referred to as on the right. The wife's arms appear on the right, but this is described as on the left.

Quartering

A son can only quarter the arms of his parents if his mother did not have any brothers. Otherwise, he just uses his father's arms.

Top: left to right Blue (azure), Red (gules);
Bottom: left to right Green (vert), Black (sable), Purple (purple).

Early coats-of-arms are not coloured (tinctured), but by the beginning of the 18thC a system of shading was used to represent colours. Green and purple are quite rare. Silver is represented by a blank shield, and gold by a shield filled with tiny dots. Blazoning a coat-of-arms can be learned with practice.

These early coat-of-arms feature crossed plumes. Although the design is not particularly artistic, they are a very fine example of early arms and they will add considerably to the price of the item.
*Like all early coats-of-arms, these are not coloured which makes it far more difficult to track down the family than with later examples.

These arms from c.1700 can be identified as those of an Earl by the coronet flanked by supporters. Although silver belonging to a peer is of added historical interest, only those engraved with royal arms command higher prices *per se*. As with the previous coat-of-arms, these are still uncoloured.

These arms from 1714 feature Baroque strapwork which was fashionable at this period. This example is made more interesting because the arms are those of a widow – identifiable by the fact that they are placed within a lozenge. Although there are considerably fewer items of silver with the arms of a widow, such pieces do not command higher prices.
*A lozenge shape tied with a ribbon at the top indicates an unmarried woman.

This is a typical coat-of-arms of the 1730s. The high quality of this design would significantly increase the price of a piece.

The asymmetrical pattern of these arms is typical of those dating from the middle of the 18thC. They usually feature similar flowers and shells and can be very pretty, adding quite considerably to the value.

These arms are a little later and reflect the rococo influence popular at the time. The design is less restrained than the previous one. This example is particularly interesting as it features a baronet's badge at the top of the arms (represented by a hand).

The heart-shaped shield is a typical feature of arms dating from c.1780 and existed with many variations.

By the end of the 18thC arms appeared with mantling and shoulder spurs. These can be very effective, particularly if the decoration is bright-cut.

These arms from 1823 are the ultimate coat-of-arms for a peer and are typical of those that appear on the grandest pieces of silver at this time. The owner has a double-barrelled name which is represented by two crests.

Although these Victorian arms feature leafy mantling it is quite different from that on examples from earlier in the century.

Crests

Smaller pieces of silver are usually engraved with crests rather than coats-of-arms. The important difference between a crest and a coat-of-arms is that a crest may be shared by anything up to 20 families whereas a coat-of-arms is traceable to one particular family, or even one particular man and wife.

*Crests are sometimes accompanied by a motto. On English examples the motto is below the crest, on Scottish examples it is above.

Initials

Some early silver is engraved with three initials within a triangle. The upper initial usually represents the family surname, and the lower two are the initials of the first names of the man and wife. Such pieces were often given as wedding presents.

Replacement and erasure of arms

When silver changed hands, the new owners sometimes erased the existing coat-of-arms and replaced it with their own. This leaves the metal thin and reduces the value, sometimes considerably. If the silver is too thin to be re-engraved, a new coat-of-arms is sometimes engraved onto the opposite side. Some arms are removed and not replaced.

*To see if a coat-of-arms has been removed push with the thumbs on the suspected area to see if it dents.

*Sometimes new arms have been added to an earlier cartouche. These can be identified by the sharper feel of the engraving.

*If a new cartouche has been let in to an existing piece of silver the solder line will appear if one breathes on the suspect area.

Condition

Any repair will lower the value of silver unless the piece is very rare. Damage is often caused by poor design, such as the feet being too small for the body, or the piece being too heavy for the base. If damage has been repaired with silver solder it can sometimes be difficult to spot. More often, lead is used in repairs, and this can be unsightly and is detrimental to the value.

*Feet are particularly susceptible to damage and are often pushed up into the base.

*Articles with handles are also vulnerable – the metal of the body is often pulled away by the handle. Handles which have come unsoldered can be resoldered in the same place without leaving a repair mark.

*Hinges are difficult to repair because of the expansion and contraction of the metal.

*Pierced decoration is very prone to damage, so always check carefully.

*If hollow-ware items such as teapots and coffee pots have been repaired using heat the inside will be a bright shiny colour.

CANDLESTICKS

A George III candlestick; Thomas Hening, London; 1776

Early candlesticks are rare, and hardly any appear on the market from before the Restoration of the Monarchy in 1660. Many candlesticks were melted down for coin during the Civil War and this resulted in a physical shortage of silver in the late 17thC. As a result, any candlesticks from this period are disproportionately light because they were hammered up from sheet metal. By the end of the 17thC candlesticks were cast, and this method of production, expensive in both technique and resources, was used until the 1770s when developments in mechanization brought about loaded examples stamped out from sheet (see p. 187). Cast candlesticks continued to be made in London on a reduced scale after this date, but very rarely in the provinces. Cast candlesticks are stronger than ones hammered from sheet. They tend to be more desirable than loaded ones and command higher prices.

Nozzles, which are detachable and stop the wax pouring down the stem of the candlestick, became a regular feature in the 1740s. They usually conform in outline to the base of the candlestick and have the same decoration.

Later 17thC candlesticks have fluted columns. However, although candlesticks got progressively taller, there are few variations from the taper or baluster stem apart from a number of mid-18thC roccoco flights of fancy with figural stems, some of which were in the form of a harlequin.

As far as American production of candlesticks is concerned very few pairs of candlesticks have survived from the 18thC and early 19thC. This is surprising considering the financial success and high standard of living enjoyed by those living on the Eastern seaboard, and the obvious need for candle lighting until other methods were discovered.

Candelabra were generally made in the same form as candlesticks. Examples from the beginning of the 18thC are rare and most date from the last quarter of the century onwards. In order to make candelabra more affordable, a number were made with Sheffield Plate branches, and these are still less expensive to buy today and provide a more affordable alternative to all-silver examples.

Chamber sticks from the early 18thC have survived in large numbers. The earlier ones, which are rare today, have the best practical features – a broad handle to give a good grip and a wide platform to catch the drips as the bearer went up to bed. Travelling chamber sticks were also made, but like cased individual beakers which came with spice containers and a knife, fork and spoon, these are rare despite their usefulness. A number were still being made at the end of the last century.

Candles with self consuming wicks were not introduced until the 19thC, so up until this time snuffers and their stands were essential. It is again surprising how few have survived compared to the huge numbers that would have been made – after all, every household with silver candlesticks would have had a need for silver snuffers. Most date from the 18thC onwards. Early examples have a simple scissor action but from the middle of the 18thC various ingenious arrangements were made in an attempt to keep the severed wick in the box. Snuffers were made by specialists, so that although they were made with stands, trays or to fit in the slotted sconces of chamber sticks, the makers of the snuffers are almost invariably different to that of the tray. Small snuffers' trays are usually decorative and well-made and are sought after in their own right (see p. 44-45).

With all candlesticks, candelabra, chambersticks and snuffers, quality and relative weight are important, whether you prefer the plain early 18thC styles or the exuberance of George IV and later examples. Remember that loaded candlesticks are artificially heavy and avoid any items in poor condition. A number of cast candlesticks have been faked by simply taking another casting, reproducing everything including the marks; any pair of candlesticks with marks in precisely the same place on each stick is very suspect. Right from the very start of production candlesticks were made in pairs or sets and despite the passage of time very few appear singly. If they do, there is a substantial reduction in value compared to the price paid for multiples. A genuine pair must be made by the same maker at the same date.

EARLY CANDLESTICKS 1
(BEFORE 1800)

*One of a pair of mid-18thC cast candlesticks; John Cafe;
ht 10in (25.5cm); value code D*

**Identification checklist for a typical mid-18thC
candlestick**
1. Is the form relatively simple and robust?
2. Are decorative elements fairly simple, perhaps including rope or circular borders or shell motifs?
3. Do the casting marks line up at the seams? (If not it could indicate the piece has been taken apart.)
4. Does it have a detachable nozzle? (If so, it was made from the 1740s onwards.)
5. Are any borders or facets worn or rounded?
6. Is it fully marked under the base or at the foot of the column?
7. Are there in addition marks on the sconce and also on the nozzle?
8. Does it measure between 6in (15cm) and 10in (25.5cm) high?
9. When lifted up does it feel relatively heavy?

Early candlesticks
The earliest English silver table candlesticks date from before the first half of the 17thC, during the reign of Charles I (1625-1649), but these are very rare. Any American candlesticks are also very rare.

Condition
Throughout the 17thC and first half of the 18thC candlesticks fulfilled a functional rather than decorative role. They were made in vast numbers in simple practical shapes and were used daily. Most survive in pairs rather than

18

singly. Because of the regular usage to which most were subjected it is not surprising that they are often in poor condition. In many cases, well-worn candlesticks were melted down and refashioned, another reason for the scarcity of early examples.

Typical characteristics
Throughout the 18thC candlesticks became progressively taller. The one in the main picture measures 10in/25.5cm, a typical size for a mid-18thC piece. Those made early in the century usually measure about 6in/15cm, and by the end of the century they had doubled in size to about 12in/30.5cm.

Mid-18thC candlesticks
The candlestick featured in the main picture has a detachable nozzle to prevent the molten wax from dripping down the sides of the stick. These were not introduced until the 1740s; earlier 17thC candlesticks which are illustrated on this page did not have nozzles.
* The shell corners on the base of the candlestick in the main picture were a popular decorative motif of the period. Other types of corners on bases are:
* plain square
* angled
* crescent-shaped.

This 17thC candlestick is of the early sheet metal type, made from sections soldered together. Compared with cast examples it feels relatively light for its size. Sheet metal sticks are especially vulnerable to damage (because of the thinness of the metal) so

examples in good condition such as this are very rare.

Manufacture
During the reign of Charles II (1660-1685) silver was in relatively short supply and candlesticks were produced from thinner sheet metal (see below left). Towards the end of the 17thC as silver supplies increased, casting, the technique used to make the candlestick in the main picture, became the most usual method of manufacture. Early cast examples tend to be smaller than those made from sheet metal. Casting continued to be used until the 1770s when improved mechanization made stamping candlesticks from finer gauge metal more economical.

The high quality of this late 17thC cast candlestick is reflected in its refined decoration. The gadroon borders were popular at this period and can be seen on many similar sticks. However, the masks and strapwork decoration on the central stem and base of the nozzle are an indication of superior quality. As this stick is cast it has survived in far better condition than earlier examples which were hammered from sheet metal.

Marks
Candlesticks made from sheet metal are often marked at the bottom of the column, rather than under the base as in later cast versions. Early cast candlesticks, (see above) were sometimes marked in the same way.

EARLY CANDLESTICKS 2

Plainer styles with very little decoration became fashionable at the beginning of the 18thC. This typical early 18thC candlestick made by Anthony Nelme is much simpler in style than the example on the previous page. The faceted baluster shape of the central column is unadorned apart from the contemporary engraved coat-of-arms on the base.
* The slight rounding of the edges on the base and central column show that this stick has been subjected to some wear and tear. Sharp faceting is an indication that the piece has not been so well-used, and such pieces will command a premium.

By 1725-30 candlesticks, such as this one by William Cafe, became taller and the casting was more elaborate than on earlier examples. Cast candlesticks should always be carefully examined for flaws such as cracks which occurred during their manufacture as if present these will reduce the value.
*The marks on either side of the seam where the piece was joined should match up; if not it could indicate the candlestick has at some stage been opened out and tampered with.

The shape of the nozzle can help with dating. On earlier candlesticks the design of the nozzle followed that of the base (see left). Later in the 18thC square-based candlesticks with circular nozzles became popular. This is a particularly fine example and was made c.1759 by John Carter, a prolific maker of candlesticks. Solid and well-made, it is simply adorned with gadrooning which makes it one of the most sought-after and expensive types of 18thC candlestick around.

Important 18thC makers
The gilt candlesticks illustrated on the opposite page were made by Thomas Pitts, a well-known London maker of candlesticks. Other makers famous for candlesticks in the early part of the century were the Gould family and the Cafe family. In the second half of the century John Scofield became renowned for his fluting on candlesticks and his elegant designs which are highly sought-after today.
*Some candlestick makers supplied wares to other makers who occasionally overstruck their own marks.

These George III silver-gilt candlesticks, made in 1772, reflect the influence of contemporary French style. They are almost identical to the candlesticks below, which were made by Robert-Joseph Auguste in Paris only a year earlier.

18thC French candlesticks

English candlesticks made in imitation of French examples are worth much less than the French original because surviving French candlesticks are far rarer; those below are worth four times the value of the English "copies" above. The scarcity of French examples is partly due to the fact that before 1789 much French

silver had to be melted down to pay for a series of wars. French candlesticks tended to be made in a greater variety of shapes and use a far wider range of decorative motifs.

Taper sticks

Taper sticks mirror the styles of their larger counterparts. They are smaller versions of candlesticks which were used primarily on a writing desk for holding a taper to melt sealing wax.

This is the most commonly-found type of taper stick, and dates from c.1730. Loaded taper sticks are slightly taller but the difference in height as the century progressed is minimal.
*Like candlesticks, taper candlesticks from the 1740s onwards have a separate nozzle.

Collecting

Taper sticks are nowhere near as common as candlesticks, and consequently they are keenly sought-after by collectors. They are nearly always sold singly; pairs therefore command a premium and may cost as much as a full-sized pair of the same date.

Condition

Although not usually subjected to the same wear as candlesticks, taper sticks are small, delicate and can be vulnerable to damage which reduces their value.

Marks

Marks on later 18thC candlesticks are often stamped in a line on the side of the base, as seen on the example on the previous page. The nozzle should also be marked with at least the maker's mark and the sterling lion passant.
*Taper sticks are almost invariably marked underneath the base, in each corner on square-based examples and in a cluster on ones with circular bases.

A loaded candlestick; John Carter, London;
1760, ht 9⅜in (24cm), value code D

Identification checklist for a later candlestick (between c.1750-1800)

1. Is the candlestick cast or loaded?
2. Can the correct marks be seen on the base and nozzle?
3. Are there any holes on the base and column, caused by stretching on areas of high-relief decoration? (This reduces value considerably.)
4. Is there any damage to the leafage?
5. Does the height seem correct for the date of the piece?
6. Is any loading intact?
7. Does the candlestick rattle when shaken. (If so the loading is loose in the column.)

Loaded candlesticks

Mechanization developed during the Industrial Revolution resulted in a proliferation of machine-made loaded candlesticks made in huge numbers to meet the growing demands of the newly affluent merchant classes. The amount of metal used to make a loaded candlestick was far less than for a cast one, so later candlesticks were significantly lower in price when made, and are still not as desirable or valuable today as cast examples. Mass-produced, loaded candlesticks were also made in Europe although because of continual political unrest, perhaps the majority of 18thC versions which survive are from Britain. Cast candlesticks of finer quality continued to be made throughout the late 18th and 19thC.

Centres of production

Most loaded candlesticks were made in the industrial centres of Birmingham and Sheffield where the machinery was located, and after the opening of assay offices in these two cities, production of loaded candlesticks increased significantly. The candlestick in the main picture is a very early example of a loaded candlestick. The style takes the form of a Corinthian column which was to remain popular throughout the 18thC and beyond. Later candlesticks had rounded bases. Occasionally loaded candlesticks made in Birmingham or Sheffield were shipped down to London where they were re-marked with the familiar London hallmark.

Beware

The metal rod with which a loaded candlestick is weighted is held in place by pitch or plaster of Paris. Sometimes this substance begins to disintegrate inside the silver skin, in which case it will rattle if gently shaken.

This fine-quality cast candlestick can be dated to c.1790 because of the reeded or thread borders which became fashionable at this time. The silversmith has taken advantage of the wide spreading base to include a full coat-of-arms rather than a simple crest. The

refined quality of the candlestick is evident in both the style and the restrained decoration. The fact that it was made using the casting process will greatly increase the value.

Repairs

A slightly bent cast candlestick can easily be repaired by a silversmith but this is not true if the stick is loaded as the internal pitch is plaster of Paris and the iron rod would have to be removed before any repairs can take place. Afterwards everything has to be put back and this is time consuming and expensive. The same is true for sticks with defective loading. The metal on a loaded stick is also fairly thin and this makes any solder repairs more difficult.

A popular innovation introduced at the turn of the 19thC was the telescopically extending candlestick. This example, made in Sheffield by Thomas and Daniel Leader in 1800, is 10in (25.5cm) high when fully extended. These candlesticks were chiefly produced in Sheffield, as was this example, and were always made using the loaded technique. Large numbers of plate telescopic candlesticks were also made. *Telescopically extending candlesticks were not made for more than about ten years.

Condition

It is important to check that the telescopic mechanism is still working and will hold the candle at any height as it is very difficult to get a defective one repaired.

LATER CANDLESTICKS 2

19thC candlesticks
By the middle years of the 19thC silversmiths looked increasingly to the past for their inspiration. By the end of the century manufacturers were eagerly copying any previous style from the 18thC that they thought suitable, in both larger and smaller versions than the originals. The styles were also applied to the manufacture of candelabra (see p.29).

Few cast candlesticks were made during the later 19thC because the process became prohibitively expensive compared with the new mechanized manufacturing techniques. Surface decoration became increasingly important and elaborate throughout this period, in keeping with the Victorian love of covering plain surfaces with excessive decoration.

This characteristically lavish loaded candlestick was made in Sheffield by Waterhouse, Hodson & Co. in 1823. Made in the neo-rococo style popular at this time, almost the entire surface of the piece is encrusted with elaborately-chased foliate scrolls and flower heads; the swirling style of decoration is further emphasized by the undulating shape of the central column.

The decoration on this loaded candlestick, made in Sheffield in 1815 by the prolific maker Kirkby, Waterhouse & Co, is relatively restrained for the Regency period. However, there are areas of high relief and these should be checked carefully for wear.
*Stamping is vulnerable to damage caused by the stretching of the silver sheet, so candlesticks such as the one illustrated here and most other examples should be carefully checked for holes in the decoration.

This figural candlestick was made in 1845 by Elkington & Co. Similar examples exist in plate. It shows a reversion to simpler forms compared to the previous examples and includes natural leafy motifs.

Many loaded candlesticks in the form of a column and with a stepped square base were made from the 1890s onwards.

The classical style, as interpreted by Robert Adam and his followers, provided a popular source of inspiration for silversmiths in the 19thC. This silver gilt candlestick uses many popular Adam motifs, including:
*rams' masks
*urns
*floral garlands.

Authenticity
If there are any signs of wear on the decoration, the gilding could have been applied at a later date and this is less desirable.

Although the basic shape of later examples is constant, considerable variations occur in the complexity of borders, the decoration of the capital and the height.

Collecting
Although popular with collectors, these candlesticks are readily available so any damage is unacceptable.
*Check particularly for damage to the corners.

Figural candlesticks
The workshop of Charles & George Fox was renowned for its production of good-quality, decorative pieces of silver throughout

the Victorian period. This pair of figural candlesticks, depicting a rustic couple are typically well-made, with some fine detailing on the skirt and bodice.

Figural candlesticks continued to be produced throughout the 19thC and beyond. Among other variations which appear on the market are:
*similar figures as those shown on the left, but in the form of two-light candelabra
*other rustic subjects such as shepherds and shepherdesses, and gardeners.
*Pairs usually represent a male and female figure, rather than two identical ones.

CHAMBER STICKS

*A George III chamber stick; Ebenezer Coker;
1763; 6in (15.5cm) diam.; value code D*

Identification checklist for an 18thC chamber stick
1. Is the pan marked in a line underneath?
2. Are the detachable parts (the extinguisher and nozzle) marked with the same marks?
3. Does the border on the pan and nozzle match?
4. Have there been any repairs made to the feet or handles?
5. Is there any sign of a crest having been removed from the pan or extinguisher?

Chamber sticks

Chamber sticks were made to hold a candle to light the way to bed and consequently they have been made in considerable numbers. Early ones from the end of the 17thC have flat handles, but these are exceptionally rare as probably not many were made at this time; most chamber sticks date from the second half of the 18thC and they disappear completely as gas lighting was introduced. Some of them must have been made in sets as all members of a family would need one. Plated examples were often made and these are usually very elaborate, with some having a glass shade to protect the flame against the wind; these shades do not often survive. Because chamber sticks have been used so much they tend not to be in good condition. They are usually sold singly, but any sold in pairs will fetch a premium.

Typical features

Borders on the pans of chamber sticks tend to follow those found on corresponding salvers of the time (see pp. 46-49); the gadroon and shell border on the stick in the main picture is the same as that found on salvers from the same period.

Condition

Conical extinguishers such as the one in the main picture are particularly vulnerable to damage and may have been replaced in a similar style. The handle can be torn away from the body, the hook from which the extinguisher hangs may detach itself, and the socket on the side of the sconce can be damaged; check all these areas carefully.
*Considering that most chamber sticks have undergone extensive and heavy use, a surprisingly large amount have survived in reasonable condition.

From c.1720 the ring or scroll handle was standard on chambersticks; it often had a slot to take a conical extinguisher.

This chamber stick by John White was made in 1727 and is one of the earliest examples likely to be found. It is marked on the top in the pan, unlike later examples which are marked underneath (in many cases early marks have been rubbed thin). As usual, the border conforms to salvers of the period, and is plain, simple and moulded. Early examples such as this did not have a nozzle.
*The slot in the centre is for an extinguisher, probably of the scissor type, but surprisingly, these were made separately and by different makers.

This chamber stick was made by Paul Storr in 1828. It is unusual for chamber sticks to be in silver gilt and this will add to the value, providing the gilt is in good condition and the decoration and marks are perfect; if they are not it is likely that the gilding has been added later which is not very desirable. The fancy border exactly echoes that on the salvers of the time.
*Paul Storr's name doubles the value of this piece.
*It is important that chamber sticks are fully marked as inkstands were made with chamber sticks attached and sometimes these may be sold separately, in which case they will only be part-marked, although they will of course be smaller.
*Very occasionally you will find chamber sticks in a different form. On some 18thC and 19thC examples the candles were held by reclining figures.

The gadroon border on this Sheffield chamber stick from 1810 appeared on a lot of silver from 1760 onwards. Silversmiths in Sheffield had to sacrifice quality in order to offer goods at a lower price than those with a London hallmark. Consequently, this example is likely to be lighter that its London counterpart (confirmed by the fact that it does not sit evenly on its base). The border is likely to be hollow and stamped rather than cast which will also reduce its weight. There are also signs of repair where the handle joins the body. On later chamber sticks like the one illustrated here the snuffer is attached to the handle.

From the last quarter of the 18thC onwards chamber sticks were occasionally made in travelling sets. These could be taken apart and screwed together or, as in this example, they came in a fitted case with holes into which they slotted. The box was also fitted to take to scissor snuffers, although these would have been supplied by a different maker. All the parts should be marked. These are rare and their value is increased by their novelty.
*Some examples have hinged candle sockets.

CANDELABRA

A pair of three-branch candelabra; John Scofield; 1780; ht 21½in (54) cm; value code B

Identification checklist for candelabra
1. Are all detachable pieces marked? The branches should be fully marked.
2. Does the design of the sconce, branch and candlestick all match each other?
3. Are the branches intact?(It is virtually impossible to repair broken loaded arms.)
4. If the candlestick is cast is its base loaded? (A common way of adding extra weight needed for stability.)
5. Is there any evidence of cracking below the sconce or at the base of the stem?

Candelabra
Candelabra dating from earlier than the late 18thC are very exceptional. Candelabra follow the same forms and styles as can-dlesticks. Most were made in pairs and had detachable branch-es that could be cast or loaded, and which fitted into the sconce at the top of the central column.

Early ones had two arms, by the end of the 18thC three were usual, and during the 19thC candelabra with up to five or more arms were made. Candelabra were always several times more expensive than candlesticks and were produced in lesser quantities. Many have not been subjected to the same wear as candlesticks and therefore they can usually be found in reasonable condition.

Marks
Every detachable part (ie every branch, sconce and nozzle) should be marked with the silver standard and maker's mark.

Typical features
The three-branch candelabra in the main picture were made by John Scofield, a well-known maker, in 1780. They measure 21½in (54cm) high. Sizes became progressively taller throughout the 18thC, reaching their peak in the Regency period. During the later part of the 19thC, following the introduction of gas-lighting, sizes tended to diminish slightly. Decoration is identical to that which would be found on candlesticks of the same date; the beaded border and fluting are typical of the late 18thC.

stem grew too high and the nozzle too wide to hold a candle.
* Check that the branches are, as here, made by the same maker as the stem, at around the same time. Occasionally candelabra had branches made by different makers and these are substantially less desirable.

Massively proportioned silver gilt candelabra are typical of the Regency period. These two were made by Paul Storr for Rundell, Bridge & Rundell. If they are correctly marked by Storr on all the individual parts, they could be worth twice as much as if they were by a less sought-after name. Each separate part should be marked identically.

Mid-18thC candelabra such as these made in 1749/52 by John Cafe are very rare. Value is increased by their unusually elaborate decoration.
* The decoration of the different parts of the candelabra should match, to indicate that everything belongs together. Here the shape of the sconces reflects the shape of the base and the scrolls on the base are mirrored in the decoration of the branches.
* On these early candelabra the branches could be removed and the central stem used as a candlestick. On later ones this dual usage was impossible because the

These candelabra were mass-produced from the late 19thC to c.1914. Although inexpensive compared with earlier versions, they are still sought-after for their decorative appeal and are often bought singly as centrepieces. They are easily damaged and repairs can be expensive and poor. Check for splits in the central column, cracking to arms and holes in beaded borders.

CHRONOLOGY OF STYLES

The typical 17thC candlestick is raised from sheet metal and has a cluster column stem. This style was followed towards the end of the century by the cast candlestick, which continued in production until after the middle of the 18thC when improved mechanization brought about the intrduction of loaded cnadlesticks stamped from sheet.

Candlesticks became taller as the 18thC progressed, starting relatively low, at about 6in or 7in (15cm or 18cm), rising to 10in (25cm) in the 1750s, and going up to 12 in (30.5cm) by the start of the 19thC; Victorian candlesticks were slightly shorter at about 10 in (25.5cm).

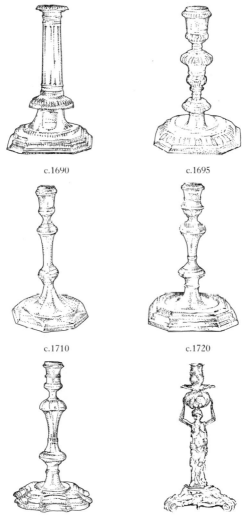

c.1690

c.1695

c.1710

c.1720

c.1735

1760

Nozzles, which are detachable and stop the wax pouring down the stem of the candlestick, became a regular feature in the 1740s. They usually conform in outline to the base of the candlestick and have the same decoration.

Tapersticks were made from the reign of Queen Anne. They tend to follow the style of candlesticks of the period. Unlike candlesticks they are acceptable singly and pairs are rare

Illustrated below is a selective representation of the changing styles of candlesticks, beginning at the start of the 17thC and going through to the middle of the 19thC. The drawings should provide a useful guide to dating and identifying the many different styles available to the collector.

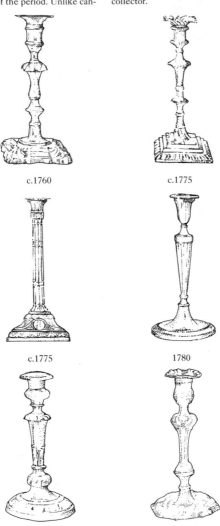

c.1760

c.1775

c.1775

1780

c.1810

c.1820

DINING SILVER

A soup tureen and stand, Paul Storr, c.1810

Silver tableware ranges from rare and expensive soup tureens and sets of plates to everyday necessities like salt cellars. Also covered in this section are snuffers as although these are not strictly dining silver, they were made by many of the same makers.

Meat plates are particularly popular with collectors. Large quantities have survived from the beginning of the 18thC because many were made to satisfy the demands of relatively wealthy familes. Meat plates command high prices and because soup plates are used far less often, many of them have been altered into meat plates over the years. As a result soup plates are rare but despite this they are still less expensive than meat plates. Borders of plates were frequently replaced to keep abreast with contemporary fashions, and any that have been altered should be avoided – remember, technically it is illegal to own them and it is certainly an offence to sell them (see p. 11). When buying plates, those with a shell and gadroon border are popular because they are easy to match and can be made into larger sets. Plates with a plain round gadroon border are not so collectable and are less expensive. Any Queen Anne plates command a premium, even singly.

Shaped oval meat dishes were made en suite with round meat plates. Most popular are the very small and the very large. Those dating from the beginning of the 18thC are rare. From the 1750s onwards dishes were occasionally fitted with a mazarine, a pierced insert which effectively gave the dish a base suitable for serving fish from. Mazarines are rare today, but the best examples with attractive piercing and engraving are popular with collectors.

The surface of plates and dishes is always plain and any ornamentation is in the border, with crests or coats-of-arms usually engraved on the rims. On salvers and trays, however, crests and arms are a prominent central feature and on many of them the engraving is magnificent. The whole surface can also be decorated, either with engraving or flat chasing, depending on the period. Because crests and arms are so important on salvers and trays it is essential to be able to identify them and recognize any later additions as these will lower the value considerably.

Sauce boats are mostly plain apart from a crest or coat-of-arms, although there are a few very elaborate rococo examples which stand on rock-like bases and have highly imaginative handles. With the onset of neo-classicism in the 1770s sauce boats gave way to sauce and soup tureens, and from this time onwards the two were often made to match. Soup tureens are extremely expensive and anyone who can afford to buy one should be particular about condition.

Other large serving items made in silver include entrée dishes. These were made in pairs and are only collectable as such today. It is important that lids have not been mixed up within a large set as this will prevent them from sitting properly on the base.

At the more affordable end of the dining silver market are cruet frames, which were first made in c.1725. Check those with glass bottles carefully as they are particularly susceptible to damage. Also, the larger types may look impressive, but they are not very usable today. Individual salt cellars and mustard pots provide two of the most attractive and varied collecting areas in silver; particularly those dating from the Victorian period which were made in a great variety of shapes and sizes. Unfortunately, the greatest enemy of the salt cellar is salt, so be meticulous about emptying it from the container when not in use. Pepper casters from the early 18thC can be magnificent and cost thousands of pounds, but most of them are relatively simple and affordable. Remember, however, that the piercing is now too large for today's fine pepper. Mustard pots were made singly but casters and salt cellars were made in pairs and any still together fetch a premium.

Finally in this section is flatware. Here it is important for the collector to find a pattern which appeals to him or herself personally, and which can be added to or made up in the event of loss. Antique knives with loaded handles are not a practical proposition, particularly those with steel blades as these rust easily and are worth very little; modern equivalents are a far better buy. It is essential to buy flatware in good condition. It should also be heavy, stand up to wear and feel comfortable in the hand. Most expensive to buy are "straight sets", where each piece has been made at the same date by the same maker, but it is perfectly possible and far cheaper to buy in smaller groups – for example, a set of six spoons and forks. In all cases, the greater variation in the dates and makers, the cheaper the price.

PLATES

A set of twelve George III dinner plates; Paul Storr, London, 1804; 10¼in (26cm) diam.; value code A

Identification checklist for a set of dinner plates

1. Are the plates marked clearly underneath in a line?
2. Have the marks been stretched in any way?
3. Is the date of the hallmark consistent with the style of the border on the plate?
4. Is there a coat-of-arms or crest? Is it contemporary to the period of the plate?
5. Is there any evidence of a coat-of-arms or crest having been removed?
6. Are there any scratches or knife marks on the surface? If not the plates are worth considerably less as it suggests they have been over-polished.

Dinner plates
The standard dinner service comprised six dozen meat plates and two dozen soup plates, with oval meat dishes made to match in any numbers up to 30 (usually in fours for the smaller sizes, pairs for the middle sizes, and singles for the larger ones). Dinner plates today tend to be sold in dozens. The largest and smallest size

meat dish are the most popular. Dinner plates can be used on the table instead of table mats On the other hand, soup plates have little use today and consequently they are a lot less expensive, even though they are considerably rarer.
*If dinner plates are sold in less than sets of 12 there is always a fall in value.

Shapes and styles

With the exception of very early dinner plates (1710-1720) shape has altered little, and any changes have been to the borders. Earlier plates had broader borders and often these have been removed and new ones put on to bring them in line with fashion. To do this, the plate had to be re-shaped and part of the original flange put into the body. Plates were originally marked underneath in a line very close to the depression with the border and when altered it was impossible not to damage the mark, so any unmarked plates will have been reshaped. Always check marks match the style of the border.

The shell and gadroon border on the plates in the main picture is typical of those from the early 19thC onwards. Examples such as these with a wavy edge are more popular than those with plain circular outlines and are easier to match with other items.

The size of these plates at 9¼in (23.7cm) diameter suggests they may be dessert rather than dinner plates. They have a decorative tide reed border, which is not quite as desirable as the gadroon, or shell and gadroon borders found on other plates at this time.

These William III dinner plates from 1691 are the earliest style of plate to be found and are characteristically expensive. Early plates were marked by the rim of the border on the top, and the marks are clearly visible on these examples. At 9⅜in (23.6cm) diameter, early plates tend to be smaller than later examples and because they do not have an applied border, weigh considerably less. Because the mark is so close to the edge, these plates are almost impossible to alter.

*Sometimes plates are sold with their scratch weight which aids in identifying whether a border has been changed.

*Early plates up until the reign of George I nearly always have a coat-of-arms; later ones sometimes have a crest.

Meat dishes were made to match the plates of the period, but can be bought to go with items with similar borders. This dish by Paul Storr has a gadrooned, shell and foliage border, which although different to the border in the main picture, will still complement them. Collectors pay a premium for Paul Storr silver, but this is not as high on plates as on more elaborate items. Although this dish was made in 1820, the coat-of-arms is in the style of the 1760s which suggests it has been copied from an earlier piece.

*Very rarely plates have an additional royal coat-of-arms which indicates that the silver was an official issue. Such items are particularly desirable.

ENTRÉE DISHES

A Regency entrée dish and cover with plated warming stands; Paul Storr; 1811; 12½in diam.; value code A

Identification checklist for a 19thC entrée dish.
1. Do the top and bottom match? (Do they bear corresponding numbers or groups of dots?)
2. Are the top and bottom fully marked, and the handles part-marked with the lion passant and duty mark?
3. Is there a coat-of-arms, or at least a crest, covering quite a large area?
4. Is the metal thin or worn where a coat-of-arms may have been removed?
5. Does the handle fit properly?
6. On dishes with screw-in handles, is the metal damaged around the socket?
7. If there is a heater base, is the plating in good condition? Is there any bleeding from the lead due to excess heat?
8. Is the heater compartment on the base still intact?

Entrée dishes

Entrée dishes were used for keeping food on a sideboard, or for serving food at a table. The earliest ones date from the 1760s, when they were often used as salad dishes and were made without lids; lids were added later in an attempt to keep food warm. By the 1780s they were always made with lids, and tend to be oval in shape. Examples from this date are not of very good quality and are usually lightweight with handles at the ends which are prone to damage. Later ones are cushion-shaped or rectangular. The lids gradually become more domed from the Regency period onwards. Entrée dishes appear to have died out by the 1830s, at which point they were often circular in shape or reproductions of older styles.

Beware

Entrée dishes are usually sold in pairs and any single ones are worth significantly less. Each dish had a number which both the top and bottom were marked with. Frequently dishes are sold with tops and bottoms that do not match which may mean that a lid does not sit square on its base.

Heater bases

From the beginning of the 19thC many of the entrée dishes came with silver plated heater bases which were either filled with hot water or a lump of heated iron.

The example in the main picture has a plated heater base designed to hold a spirit burner. The bases have frequently been discarded, but this does not greatly alter the price of the dish.

The round shape of this entrée dish is typical of those made at the end of the reign of George IV. The scale of decoration and the heavy weight would have made it very expensive.

This early dish from 1768, made as one of a pair, was originally made without a lid to be used as a salad dish; the lid has been added over 20 years later and is marked accordingly. Also, the body is slightly smaller and lighter than that of later examples. Despite the large plain surface, this dish has only been engraved with a crest. Most entrée dishes usually have a coat-of-arms; in some cases there is a crest on one part and a coat-of-arms on the other and the two should obviously match in date.
*Wooden handles only appear on this early type of entrée dish; later ones became increasingly innovative and decorative, often in the shape of vegetables.

Damage
Occasionally the domed lid was made in Sheffield plate to save money. If this is the case, check the lid carefully for copper on the highlights and for lead on the decoration at the handle; wear can only get worse. The decoration on the entrée dish illustrated above is too elaborate for the dish to be plate. Because these dishes were cast it is difficult to damage them, although the handle is probably held on with two screws and if these are removed it is hard to put them back properly.

Marks
The base and cover should be fully marked in a straight line and should include the duty mark from 1784 onwards.
*All other detachable parts should bear the maker's mark and lion passant.

This George III entrée dish was made by Paul Storr for Rundell, Bridge & Rundell in 1811 and shows a progression from earlier borders on the cover of the dish to a collar. Despite the elaborate decoration, there is still space for a decorative coat-of-arms on the cover. The shape of the body is now cushion-shaped, rather than rectangular, and the top is significantly more domed than on earlier examples.
*The elaborate detachable handle is typical of Storr's work – similar handles appear on soup tureens made by him (see pp. 42-43).

This early Victorian melon-shaped entrée dish can be found with the handles formed either as various vegetables, which appealed to Victorian taste, or with elaborately entwined handles; this example has a crest of a deer standing beneath a tree. Similar shapes were used for soup tureens of the time (see pp. 42-43). The surfaces are often plain apart from a crest, or a coat-of-arms which appears on this example.

37

SAUCE BOATS

A sauceboat on three feet; Smith & Sharp; 1763; value code D (for a pair)

Identification checklist for a mid-18thC sauceboat

1. Is the form a typical bulbous boat shape?
2. Does it stand on three feet?
3. Has the body been made in one piece (and is it therefore seamless)?
4. Is any decoration on the body confined to a crest or coat-of-arms?
5. Does the border on the rim both decorate and reinforce the body? (Those with waved edges often have splits in them.)
6. Is the scroll or flying scroll handle securely attached to the body?
7. Are the marks clearly defined?

Typical features

Although sauces had been served with food in the 17thC the earliest sauceboats date from the reign of George I (1714-1727). The sauceboat in the main picture is a typical mid-18thC example, with a plain fairly deep body, three feet and a scroll handle. Decoration is characteristically restrained – confined to a gadrooned border that serves to strengthen the lip, and shells adorning the feet.

The development of later styles in sauceboats was largely determined by practical considerations. Silver is an efficient conductor of heat, but this also means that hot contents grow cold quickly especially in sauceboats with feet.

Collecting

Sauceboats were usually made in pairs and single ones are far less desirable – worth a third to a quarter of the price of a pair.

Early sauceboats were extremely simple and had no feet, only a central stand. This example, made in c.1724 by Joseph Clare, is in the earliest style, which had a shallow boat-shaped body with handles on either side in the centre and pouring spouts at each end. Typically, it is completely undecorated, with a plain border and no adornment on the handles. These do not pour well.

Crests or arms were frequently the only form of decoration to be found on the body of 18thC sauceboats. This is one of a good-quality pair made in 1730. However the crest has a halo around it which indicates that a previous crest has been removed. The extent to which this will reduce the value depends on how thin the silver has become.
*Evidence of replaced crests is easier to see on silver that has not been recently cleaned because the silver in the area that has been erased oxidizes (tarnishes) at a different rate from that of the rest of the body. Puffing heavily on a suspect area can also help to reveal replaced crests.

Towards the end of mainstream production of sauceboats (c.1745-1765) central feet returned to favour, the bowl tended to be deeper and the spout wider and more raised. Decorative borders became more noticeable, as can be seen on this sauceboat made by Thomas Heming of London in 1769. It has a fairly elaborate gadroon, foliate and shell border applied to the rim and around the foot, and a double-scroll handle.

Marks
Marks are usually placed under the body in a straight line. Some from the 1770s are marked under the lip, where they often get rubbed. Those on a cental foot can be marked either on the rim or on the inside of the foot.

Damage
The feet on sauce boats are vulnerable to damage and may get bent out or pushed into the body.

Later sauceboats
The sauceboat returned to favour after the Regency period and continued to be made throughout Victorian times. Most 19thC sauceboats were made in imitation of 18thC styles, although one or two highly elaborate and original Regency pieces were produced. The sauceboats below were made in a set of six by

Robert Garrard in 1826. Their outstanding features include a heavy cast foot, applied shell and strapwork motifs and leaf-capped scroll handles. In the 19thC many sauceboats were made as part of ceramic dinner services. The reproductions made at the end of the 19thC and later are, with few exceptions, copies of mid-18thC examples on three feet.

SAUCE TUREEENS

A late 18thC sauce tureen; Robert Sharp;
1791; value code D

Identification checklist for sauce tureens from c.1775-1800

1. Is the shape elegant and refined?
2. Is the lid marked on a flange with the maker's mark and, possibly, a lion passant and duty mark?
3. Does the lid fit snugly into the base?
4. Do any numbers or dots on the body match those on the lid?
5. Does any crest on the body match those on the lid?
6. If the lid has a finial is it attached with a screw rather than solder? (A sign of quality.)
7. Has the foot remained in its original position?
8. If there is any decoration is it relatively restrained?
9. Is there a central pedestal foot, and has it been pushed up into the body?

Sauce tureens

Lidded sauce tureens became popular in the 1770s, presumably in an attempt to keep gravy hot. The tureen in the main picture was made in 1791 and shows the elegant two-handled shape which is typical of the late 18thC. Sauce tureens continued to be popular until the early 19thC when they were replaced by ceramic ones.

Like sauce boats, sauce tureens were made in pairs or larger sets, often to match soup tureens (see pp.42-3). If the sauce tureen has originally been part of an extensive suite it may have an identifying number or series of dots on the lid, which should correspond with those on the body. If the lid does not fit well it could have become separated from the correct base and the value may be affected.

Decoration

Decoration on classical-style tureens remained relatively restrained, usually confined, as in the tureen in the main picture, to a gadrooned border or reeding. Some more ornate examples were made with bud finials and applied swags, but these are much rarer and are always expensive (see right). Crests or insignia on the body should match those on the lid.

*On the tureen above the ducal coronet surmounts the monogram showing the tureen's illustrious origins.

This pair of tureens from 1777 by Makepeace and Carter demonstrates the trend in earlier examples to have four feet rather than one central foot which began to appear c.1780 (see below). Decoration is relatively heavy and elaborate – here the detachable cover finial is in the shape of a pomegranate and there are foliate scroll side handles and shells on the tops of the legs. The gadroon border strengthens the rim of the base. Other borders popular on 18thC sauce tureens are:
*thread
*beaded

Condition
Separately applied parts can be particularly vulnerable to damage. Points in particular to check for are:
* legs pushed up into the base
* handles pulled away from the lid – especially when soldered rather than screwed on
* handles that are cracked
*borders that have split.

Marks
All separate parts – cover, handle and base – should be marked at least with the maker's mark. A full set of marks should appear on the body.

Although the tureen above, also made by Makepeace and Carter, was made only three years later than the one at the top of the page, the four feet have been

replaced by a central pedestal. The laurel and swag and ram's head decoration and ring handles exemplify the classically inspired "Adam" style popular at the time. Less expensive versions have chased swags; more expensive ones have cast and applied decoration and are heavier. There is little room for arms, so a small crest has been squeezed in at the bottom of the body and the lid.

This 1796 sauce tureen follows the same basic shape as the example below left but in a much simplified form. It probably weighs far less than its more elaborate counterpart and would originally have cost far less to buy. Decoration is confined to a simple reeded border. Plain surfaces such as this are more easily damaged and any dents or scratches would be clearly visible.
*There is no crest or coat-of-arms on this tureen, and the metal should be checked to make sure nothing has been erased. If the silver has not been tampered with the lack of a crest will not reduce the value.

Collecting
Shapes can affect values. The more elegant forms tend to be most sought-after by collectors. Oblong sauce tureens are not generally popular and are the least valuable.

Reproductions
In the late 19thC, heavy and ornate tureens on four feet, based on early 17thC designs, became popular once again.

41

SOUP TUREENS

An oval "boat-shaped" soup tureen; Wakelin and Taylor; 1779; value code B.

Identification checklist for a late-18thC soup tureen
1. Is the piece fully hallmarked underneath?
2. Is the lid also fully marked (less the town mark)?
3. Is the coat-of-arms contemporary, or has an old one been removed?.
4. Is there no damage to the body? (Check the body has not sunk into the base.)
5. Is there any beaded decoration? (This dates it to either c.1780 or c.1860.)
6. Does it have loop handles, pedestal foot and bats-wing fluting?

Soup tureens
Most soup tureens date from the reign of George III or later; earlier ones do exist, but anything before 1750 is very rare. They were very large and expensive and only relatively grand houses could afford them. They are usually oval, which is the most desirable shape, although oblong and circular examples do exist. Towards the end of the 18thC sauce tureens (see pp. 40-41) were made to match the soup tureen, but these sets are rare today. The handles of soup tureens tend to be more inventive than those of sauce tureens. Early soup tureens were made as singles, but later ones were occasionally made as pairs. Nearly all were made in London. Very elaborate tureens were made in the

rococo period of the 1720s and 1750s using fish and shells as decoration. The Regency period saw similarly decorative creations, using in some cases Egyptian motifs and others inspired by Napoleon's campaigns.

Liners
Soup tureens with a complicated shape were sometimes made with liners which are frequently Sheffield plate rather than silver. Silver liners are sometimes sold as 18thC dessert baskets, but can be identified because they usually have the town mark missing.

Marks
The base of the tureen will be fully marked, and the lids will have the leopard's head, maker's mark and the sovereign's head.

This oval-shaped, side handled soup tureen of 1750 is the earliest style to be found, and was produced with variations until the 1770s. Early examples such as this have four feet. The bud finial is an attractive touch; the best examples are decorated with flowers and vegetables, crustacea and other animals.

Beware
The elaborate cartouche encircles a crest which is later than the piece, so check the body for thinness where an earlier crest may have been removed.

This soup tureen from 1809 is fairly typical of Paul Storr's work, although a little less elaborate than some pieces by him. The central foot of the late 18thC was replaced by four feet in the early 19thC. Typical features include:
*lion masks on the handles and on the finial
*dolphin feet
*a decorative coat-of-arms.

Inscriptions
The inscription on the example below left marking the conquest in Java in 1811 gives it an interesting historical context which makes it desirable. Other inscriptions of a personal nature are irrelevant and will devalue the piece considerably.

Bases
This example could have been made with a large, two-handled base to which it would be attached by screws that would go up into the bottom of the feet. If the feet of a tureen have threaded holes the tureen should come accompanied by a base. A base increases the value of a tureen considerably, but examples frequently appear without them.

Damage
Even with careful use the feet are often inadequate for the size and weight of the tureen and may be pushed through the body. The finials on late-19thC tureens are often not detachable and as the cover may be quite light, the metal can become stretched or torn.

The melon shape of the pair of fine-quality tureens illustrated below was popular in the 1830s and '40s. The finial has been realistically cast and chased with artichokes and shallots, reflecting some of the vegetables which may be used in the soup. Some more unusual examples may have a heraldic finial. The base adds considerably to the weight, decorative effect and price of the tureen, as does the fact that the tureen is one of a pair, and was made by the reputable silversmith Robert Garrard.
*The base should be fully marked to correspond with the marks on the tureens.

SNUFFERS' TRAYS

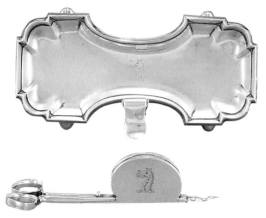

A candle snuffer and tray; James Gould;
1732; value code D (for set)

Identification checklist for 18thC-19thC snuffers' trays
1. Is the tray fully marked under the base with a mark in each corner?
2. Are any snuffers marked on both sides?
3. Are both the snuffers and tray of the same date? (The closer together in time they are, the better.)
4. If the snuffers and tray are crested, do the crests match each other?
5. Has a crest been removed from either the tray or snuffers?
6. Does the pair of snuffers still have its tip? (Any damage will reduce value.)
7. Is there any wear to the pivot on the snuffers?

Snuffers
Snuffers, of a scissor form, were used for trimming wicks which had not burnt down with the candles. They were made in substantial numbers as it was only in the 19thC that candles consumed their wicks. The earliest snuffers and trays commonly seen date from the beginning of the 1700s. Although they were probably retailed as sets, most snuffers and trays were not made by the same maker – the one illustrated above is an exception. Usually candlestick makers produced the trays (see pp. 26-27), while specialists produced the snuffers. Apart from early 18thC examples where the stand was made vertically like a candlestick (see opposite), few snuffers have their original

stands. Designs changed little between the 18th and 19th centuries. Keeping the cut wick in the top proved a problem. The most ingenious solution was to use a blade operating vertically out of line with the cut, which closed off half the box while the wick was trimmed.

Collecting
Snuffers' trays are collectable in their own right as most were well made and have usually survived in reasonable condition. Except for the candlestick variety, most are relatively inexpensive. During the 19thC silver was more often replaced by plate for snuffers and such examples are widely available and very affordable. Silver ones are far rarer.

Made in 1753 by John Cafe, one of the most prolific candlestick makers of the period, this snuffers' tray has the typical shell and scroll border also seen on salvers of the period (see pp. 46-49). It is quite solid with substantial feet. Often this type are decorated with flat chasing at either end of the tray.

The earliest type of 18thC snuffers' stand resembled a candlestick and held the snuffers upright inside the body. This one was made in 1729 by Matthew Cooper but the design is more usually found in the period from 1710-15. It was probably made at a later date to replace a lost stand or to match a pair of candlesticks. Snuffers of this type are extremely rare and among the most valuable types available.

Plain oval snuffers' trays such as the pair illustrated below, made by Paul Storr in 1809, are sometimes sold as pen trays and at other times as snuffers' trays; there is no discernible difference. Snuffers' trays of this type tend not to have feet but have handles at each end. They are frequently decorated with the opulent gadroon borders typical of the Regency period.
*The snuffers were made by James Scott of Dublin in 1810, but both the snuffers and the trays have the same crest, showing that they belong together.
*Paul Storr is one of the most revered silversmiths of the Regency period, and the trays would command a premium because of his mark.
*The tray on the left has a small dent. However, this could easily be removed and would not greatly affect value.

The hallmarks scattered in each corner on the top of this snuffers' tray are more usually positioned underneath. Surprisingly for such a small item, this early example, dating from 1714, also has a coat-of-arms in the centre of the tray. It is characteristically solidly-made and the octagonal shape will add to its desirability and increases value. Any crest or arms on the snuffers should ideally match those on the tray.

Beware
Pen trays and snuffers' trays of this shape are frequently converted into more expensive objects such as inkstands. Conversions however will not have matching marks on all the parts.

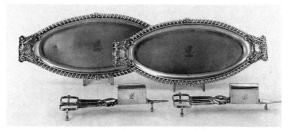

SALVERS 1

A silver salver; Robert Abercromby;
1745; 15in (38cm) diam.; value code B

Identification checklist for a mid-18thC salver
1. Is it hallmarked in a line underneath the base?
2. Are the arms original?
3. Is the decoration chased (1740s) or engraved?
4. Is the border either moulded and applied, or cast?
5. Is the silver solid?
6. Has the border remained in good condition with no splitting?
7. Does it have three cast feet rather than one central one?

Salvers
The first commonly-seen salvers date from the end of the 17thC and were used to present and serve food or drink. The earliest type had a central trumpet-shaped foot, resembling a tazza, but by the reign of George I (c.1714), the central foot was replaced by three or more small feet. Most salvers are oval or circular, as exemplified by the one above, made in 1745. Unusual salver shapes such as square and octofoil (a lobed variation of the octagonal form) are particularly sought-after and valuable.

Trays or salvers?
Nowadays small salvers are occasionally described as waiters. Current convention says that a tray should have handles (see pp. 50-51), but during the 18thC the terms for trays and salvers were interchangeable, and some large rectangular salvers were listed as trays.

Collecting
When collecting salvers, price depends primarily on the size of salver within its type, then on its relative weight and the overall condition.

Salvers with a raised central foot, as seen above, are only desirable if marked with a lion passant or a leopard's head erased (if made during the Britannia period). Most salvers of this type are decorated with a stamped or cast gadroon border. Occasionally the foot unscrews, and on the finest examples the socket is decorated with cut card work.
*Value greatly depends on size and quality.

Alterations
Sometimes the central foot has been removed and replaced with three small feet. This illegal alteration greatly reduces value but evidence of the central foot will usually remain visible on the underside of the salver.

Decoration
Most salvers had a crest or coat-of-arms engraved in a decorative cartouche in the centre and were edged by a decorative border. The formal Baroque cartouche on the salver in the main picture is a little unusual for the period, but armorials of this size, if they are original, can help with dating (see pp. 14-15).

easily on a plain flat surface such as this. The point where the base teams up to the border is especially vulnerable to splitting and should be checked for repairs.

Beware
Many 18thC salvers were re-decorated in the Victorian period. The chasing is usually broader and the style of decoration in greater relief with more elaborate motifs than would be expected in the 18thC. Salvers from the 18thC were hallmarked after the decoration so the marks will interrupt the pattern on the back. If the salver was chased after the date it was made, the pattern will go through the marks.

Borders
For a few years in the mid-18thC salvers with cast borders were popular; the border was made separately in sections and then soldered to the body and should be marked. Because the borders are cast they add considerably to the weight and are very difficult to damage.

Square-shaped salvers with four rather than three feet were popular in the 1730s – this one was made by the well-known salver maker Robert Abercromby in 1732. Imperfections show up

Particularly large salvers such as this one made by William Cripps in 1764 (26in (66cm) diam.) were reinforced with a wood backing. Although this salver has an attractive cartouche of Chinoiserie-style pagodas and trailing flowers the arms have been replaced, thus greatly reducing the value.

47

SALVERS 2

The shell and scroll border on this salver by John Carter, London 1767, evolved from the simple moulded border (seen on p. 46). The same border was also popular in a slightly more elaborate version during the Victorian period, when it was accompanied by a broad chased band of scrolls and thorns on a matted ground.

Borders
It is useful to be able to differentiate between the 18thC chasing on the salver on p. 46 and the broader later style on p. 49.

John Scofield who made this salver in 1789 was a good and popular maker. Several features add to its desirability:
*attractive bright-cut decoration
*particularly decorative and unusual border incorporating an applied leaf-tip pattern (reeding or beading would be far more usual at this time)
*good contemporary coat-of-arms with a bright cut oval frame
*large size (18½in (46cm) diam.) and heavy weight (86oz, 132dwt). The heart-shaped shield enclosing the arms is characteristic of the period.

Simpler shapes adorned with beaded (as here) or thread borders became fashionable towards the end of the 18thC. This salver by Hester Bateman made in 1784 has a cast outer border popular at this time and is typically large (18in (45.6cm) diam.) and heavy. The inner band of beading is usually stamped and may be vulnerable to damage. Sometimes there is a hole in almost every bead.

Regency salvers

Weight and quality are synonymous in Regency salvers; the most expensive are silver gilt. Chasing was extensive and many had large borders and paw feet.

The value of this elaborate Regency salver is boosted by the fact that it was made by Paul Storr, a celebrated silversmith of his day (see p. 184). Other factors affecting the value of salvers are:
*decoration – opulent cast borders like this are highly desirable
*size – large salvers are rare and sought-after
*sets – salvers were often made in pairs or larger numbers; a pair is worth more than twice a single, the premium increasing with age.

The Regency salver illustrated below was made by William Burwash in 1812 as one of a pair. It has several features typical of the period:
*a fine shell gadroon border
*flowing mantling surrounding the coat-of-arms
*paw feet
*substantial weight for size – 16in (40cm) long; 122oz (244dwt).

Removal of arms

Removed or re-engraved arms reduce value considerably. If the salver has more wear to the cartouche than to the arms the value will also be reduced. As with trays (see pp.50-51) it is difficult to remove arms without leaving a noticeable dip in the metal – however the erasure can be concealed by hammering the dip through to the back. Sometimes the centre of the salver was cut out. When well done, this can be difficult to see from the front because the engraving of the cartouche will conceal the solder line. It will be apparent from the back unless it has been concealed by plating. Removal of arms, and therefore metal, can make a salver flexible.

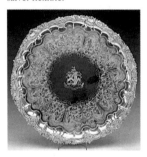

Made in 1828 by Edward Barnard & Sons, this heavily decorated salver with a broad band of chased flowers and cast border, reflects the over-embellishment typical of the 19thC. In contrast, the arms are quite restrained, perhaps due to lack of space.

TRAYS

An oval tea tray; Hannam & Crouch; London;
1806; lgth 27in (68cm); value code E

Identification checklist for late 18th-early 19thC trays
1. Is the tray marked in a line under the base with a large set of hallmarks?
2. Are the feet in proportion to the tray?
3. Is there a crest or coat-of-arms?
4. Does the border conform with the period of the tray?
5. If there is an engraved band, is this in keeping with the date of the tray?
6. Have the feet been pushed into the flat metal surface of the tray?

Trays

Trays usually have handles whilst salvers do not, although some large rectangular trays without handles were made from the early years of the 17thC, until c.1750, occasionally supported with mahogany backs to bear the weight. Few trays were made before the 1780s and most early examples are oval in shape. They tend to be larger than most salvers and became popular as teasets became fashionable. Trays were made by many of the same silversmiths who made salvers, and among the best known are Hannam & Crouch, who made the tray above, and Emes & Barnard. Border styles tend to follow those seen on salvers (see pp.46-49) and like salvers, trays became progressively more elaborate in the 19thC. Also like salvers, trays usually have feet. These need to be solid to bear the weight of the metal.

Trays of the type illustrated above were made with minor variations from c.1790 onwards. However the distinctive shape of the shield holding the arms, with its pointed top, is particularly characteristic of the early 19thC. The engraved border is also typical of this period – earlier trays usually had bright-cut borders.

Armorials

Almost all trays are engraved with a coat-of-arms, crest or inscription and one without any central motif should be regarded with suspicion. If a crest has been removed from the centre of a tray there will be a discernible dip in the metal and the value of the piece will be significantly reduced. Trays are usually thick enough for the indentation to be concealed by hammering it through to the back, leaving the surface flat. It is sometimes easier to feel the dips with the fingertips.

The simple reeded border on the tray above made by Thomas Robins of London in 1795 was popular in the 1790s. However this tray has two features which are detrimental to its value:
* a lack of an engraved decoration
* arms which are not contemporary with the tray – they have been added into an older cartouche by carefully cutting round the original engraving.

The tray illustrated below is a typical early-19thC example, and has a contemporary coat-of-arms and very elaborate foliate decoration and mantling. The considerable additional ornamentation around the handles is a desirable feature which reinforces the strength of the tray and also proves that the handles have not been added at a later date.
*Very few trays are simply centred by a crest because arms and a cartouche fill the space far more satisfactorily.
*By the start of the 19thC taking tea and coffee with friends was a very popular pastime. This led to a need for larger trays to cope with everything that was put on them. It is hard to believe that some of the largest were manageable when loaded with a comprehensive teaset.

A variation of the Regency tray popular at the end of the 19thC, was the gallery tray made in silver and plate, with low sides pierced with a trellis, topped by a gadroon or reeded border. Although in some ways more practical, the handle incorporated into the side created a weakness in the design.

Square shapes, elaborate borders and chased decoration typify trays of the William IV period and presage later Victorian examples.

This Wiliam IV tray, made by Joseph & John Angell of London in 1835 has a lavish foliate, scroll, shell and anthemion rim and is further flat chased with a broad band of foliage, fruit and scrolls. Compared with the earlier examples illustrated on these pages, there is hardly any surface left undecorated. Trays of this date are always relatively large (this one measures 28in (71cm) in length) and are highly sought-after by collectors.

Beware
Occasionally meat dishes with handles that have been added are sold as trays, these can usually be identified by their lack of feet and by the fact that the handles are not integral to the body.

CRUET FRAMES

A Warwick cruet frame;
1749; ht 8in (20cm); value code B

Identification checklist for a mid-18thC Warwick cruet
1. Is the frame marked underneath the base of the body?
2. Are the same marks visible on the bottles, caster and covers?
3. Is the handle marked with at least a lion passant and maker's mark?
4. If there is a crest, is it the same on both casters and frame?
5. Is there any damage to the piercing on the casters?
6. Are the bottles intact, and the same size?
7. Are the handles and feet in good condition?

Cruet frames
The earliest cruets were made in the 1720s. The Warwick frame in the main picture comprises a set of three casters – to hold salt, mustard and pepper – and two glass bottles for oil and vinegar. By the end of the 18thC the number of bottles and casters in a set had risen to eight or even ten in a frame. Originally, rectangular or crescent-shaped sauce labels (small versions of wine labels) would have hung round the necks of the bottles. Shapes of bottles and casters vary according to the date they were made. This set has vase-shaped bodies, which were fashionable just before the baluster shape became popular.

Marks
The body should have a full set of hallmarks; the handle, if it unscrews, should also be part-marked. Bottle mounts are frequently not marked before 1784, but should be marked thereafter.

Beware

Handles are sometimes converted into toasting forks. Incomplete marks on a toasting fork should therefore be treated with suspicion.

By the third quarter of the 18thC oil and vinegar bottles were made with decorative handles and hinged covers and casters had glass bodies. Piercing, as seen on this cruet base and casters, made in 1773 by Thomas & Jabez Daniell, should be checked very carefully for damage. The feet are especially vulnerable since they tend to have been subjected to the most stress.

This type of cruet frame was produced in large numbers during the last decade of the 18thC. Because the silver used was frequently thin and the quality poor, they are rarely seen in good condition today. The weight of the cut or faceted glass bottles contained within the frame often

damages the rather spindly feet and this greatly reduces the value. The handles on baskets of this type should be hallmarked and have a flange which is cut to hold the bottles in place.

Bottles

Bottles and their frames frequently become separated from one another and are sold individually; always check they fit the frame correctly and all match. Other points to watch for are:
*damage to bottles such as chips and cracks – this reduces value and can be very expensive or impossible to repair satisfactorily
*bottles of varying height – this could indicate a chip has been ground down on a neck and reduces value.

This more solid cruet frame was made in 1825. By this date the cruet simply comprised a tray with bottles held in a frame by a central handle. Compared with the late-18thC version on the left the feet are much more sturdy and robust, but they should still be carefully checked for damage. Some cruets of this type are decorated with crests or coats-of-arms on the surface of the tray.
* All the separate pieces – base, frame, tops and handle (if detachable) – should have matching marks.

Collecting

Cruets are popular with collectors but nowadays they tend to be used for display rather than for their original purpose and prices vary dramatically according to quality. Warwick frames are among the most desirable and rare cruets commanding the highest prices. Solid heavy cruets (like the one above) are also popular, especially if made by a premier maker, such as Paul Storr. Damaged cruets of lesser quality are available for modest sums.

SALT CELLARS

A George II salt cellar; Edward Wakelin, London; 1748; 3¼in (8cm) diam; value code D

Identification checklist for a mid-18thC salt cellar
1. Is the salt cellar marked in a group under the base?
2. Is the body free from any salt corrosion?
3. Are the feet not pushed into the body?
4. Do the feet sit squarely on the table? Is there any damage at the joints?
5. Does it have a well-fitting blue glass liner?
6. Is it one of a pair or a larger set? (Single ones are far less sought-after.)
7. Is any chased decoration applied?

Salt cellars
Early large Elizabethan salt cellars have little in common with these later versions and are today very expensive and rarely seen on the collector's market. Salt cellars were produced in large numbers from the 18thC onwards, in pairs or larger sets. They were not made to match other condiments such as pepper until the late Victorian period, although a few pierced ones made at the end of the 18thC matched mustard pots (see the one illustrated on the opposite page).

Collecting
The example illustrated in the main picture is the most common type of 18thC salt cellar. Signs which make the piece more valuable are the gadroon border around the rim, and the feet headed by lions' masks. The floral swags have been cast and applied to the body which adds considerably to the weight. The value is further helped by the thickness of the metal; a salt cellar which feels heavy in the hand is especially desirable because salt is a highly corrosive substance and may burn holes in the metal; those made of thicker metal will last longer.

Condition
Condition is particularly important when buying salt cellars. Salt should never be left in a silver salt cellar, even over night. The only protection against salt corrosion is the insertion of a glass liner, or gilding on the inside. However, even with a liner, grains of salt spill down the side and corrode the metal beneath the glass. Modest corrosion can be eradicated by covering the

spot with ammonia – if the ammonia turns blue it shows the treatment is working. Serious corrosion can only be repaired by a silversmith. If the corrosion has been polished off the base will become very thin and flexible and the marks will be worn, making it of little value at all.

This is the earliest type of salt cellar commonly seen and dates from 1693. Salts from the 17thC are usually quite heavy and have lasted in surprisingly good condition. They are sometimes sold in large sets, suggesting that rather than passing the salt, each person at the table had their own cellar; this one was from a set of six.

Trencher salts have no feet. Popular from c.1700-c.1720, they can be rectangular, circular or, as here, octagonal. Surfaces were usually left plain, but occasionally the side was adorned with a crest. Some are very light, and any with worn bowls and splits at joins should be avoided.

Salts with pierced bodies raised on four feet were made in large numbers in the 1770s, occasionally with matching mustard pots.

They remain easily available and are relatively inexpensive, depending on quality. This one is of reasonable quality with an attractive wavy rim (mirrored by its liner) and good quality ball and claw feet.
*This type of salt cellar is prone to split rims, damaged piercing and cracked or broken feet, so always check carefully.

This elegant 1790s salt cellar has several desirable features that add to its value:
*attractive fluted body
*octagonal shape
*end grips
*gilded interior (can be used without a liner).
One drawback of this style is the potential weakness at the point where the foot joins the body and this should be checked for splits.

Marks
Trenchers are usually marked in a line under the bowls, marks may be badly worn. Marks on late 18thC salt cellars may be on each corner or in a line.

These dishes are sometimes sold on their own as sweetmeat dishes, but this is actually a late 18thC salt cellar stand without its glass holder. Salts of this type are usually of reasonable weight and can be attractive if sold with their glass holder as part of a set. Individually and without their liner they are less interesting.

PEPPER CASTERS

A pepper caster; Samuel Wood;
1761; ht 6in (15cm); value code B

Identification checklist for a mid-18thC pepper caster
1. Is the caster marked under the base in a group?
2. Are there also marks on the cover?
3. Has the piercing remained intact?
4. Is the finial in good, unrestored condition?
5. If there is a coat-of-arms, is it contemporary with the date of the caster?
6. Does the join between foot and body seem secure?
7. Is the caster a tall bulbous shape?

Pepper casters
Casters were made from the late 17thC, frequently in sets of three, with one large and two smaller casters. The larger caster was used for sugar; smaller ones were for pepper. Small casters which have a design engraved on the cover but are not pierced are occasionally seen – these were for dry mustard. Mustard seed was not castable so the lid would have had to be removed to serve the contents. Casters diminished in popularity towards the end of the 18thC, when they were replaced by cruets (see pp. 52-3). Single casters are not undesirable but sets command a premium. Earlier ones are often single.

The caster in the main picture was made in 1761 by Samuel Wood, one of the best-known and most prolific caster-makers of the time. The tall, bulbous shape remained basically the same throughout the century, although the foot became progressively taller. The caster has two important features which add to its desirability:
*highly decorative piercing and engraving on the cover
*a contemporary coat-of-arms.

Marks

Marks should be found on both the body and the cover. The body tends to be marked under the base in a group, although early ones and those from the late 18thC are sometimes marked in a straight line on the body. The cover is usually marked with a lion passant and possibly a maker's mark. Covers with no marks should give cause for suspicion.

The lighthouse-shaped caster became popular in the early 18thC. The cover is attached to the base by a bayonet fitting , where two locking lugs are slotted into a flange and rotated to secure the two pieces. This caster was made by John Smith in 1703. Such early casters tend to be quite heavy and solid in appearance because pepper was expensive and merited a good holder. This one is worth several times more than the one in the main picture.

Because octagonal shaped casters are highly decorative, usually early, and rarer than circular ones, they always command a premium. This 1718 caster made by Charles Adam, a well-known maker, would be highly sought-after and, in perfect condition, worth about 50 per cent more than a circular one. The top now has a bezel (rim) and this is where the cover marks should be.

Irish provincial silver is avidly collected, not only in Ireland, but also on the international market, and this robust kitchen pepper, made by William Clark of Cork, would be highly sought-after. Casters of this type are termed kitchen peppers because they have a handle to enable the cook to season the food more easily. Peppers of this distinctive shape date from before c.1730 and are relatively scarce. This one is fairly simple in form; some have more decoratively pierced covers.

Bun peppers, so-called because of the shape of the cover, were produced throughout the 18thC; this one was made in 1731 by John Gamon, a prolific maker. Bun peppers are smaller than most others, measuring around 3in (7.5cm), and were among the least expensive casters.
*Bun peppers are usually marked in the piercing. As there is no bezel on the cover, the tops fall off easily, and many were lost and replaced. If the cover is not contemporary with the base the pepper is best avoided.

MUSTARD POTS

*An octagonal bright-cut mustard pot;
1792; value code E*

Identification checklist for a late 18thC mustard pot
1. Does the piece bear a full set of hallmarks on the body in a line?
2. Is there a maker's mark and lion passant on the cover?
3. If the pot was made after 1784, is there also a sovereign's head mark?
4. Does the liner fit well?
5. Has the finial remained intact? (If it has been torn off the value is reduced.)
6. Is the hinge in a good state of repair?
7. Does the silver on the side or cover seem thinner than the rest of the body? (This could indicate an erased crest and reduces value.)

Mustard Pots
Mustard was a dry condiment and served in casters (see p. 56) until the middle of the 18thC. Mustard pots became popular from c.1765-70. Early pots were usually fitted with blue glass liners which was easier to wash than silver. The pots were made as individual items in a huge range of shapes and sizes. Condiment sets with matching mustard, salt and pepper were not made until the late Victorian period. Fitted cases found with some later sets are useful for storage, look good on display, and add to the value.

Collecting
Mustard pots are a popular collecting area and vary greatly in price, depending on the desirability of their style. Octagonal pots, such as the one in the main picture, command a premium. Bright-cut engraved decoration of this type also boosts the value. Figural and novelty pots are also popular with today's collectors and can fetch exceptional prices (see opposite).

Marks
The body should have a full set of hallmarks, either in a group on

the base, in a line on the body, or in a curve round the base. Lids should be separately marked with maker's mark and lion passant; pieces made after 1784 should also have the sovereign's head.

Liners

Original liners have a large star cut in the base. Many pots have replacement liners; these are acceptable and do not greatly affect the price, provided the liner fits snugly.

Spoons

Mustard spoons were made by spoonmakers, a specific trade distinct from makers of mustard pots. Spoons were usually bought separately, but they were sometimes engraved to match the pot.

The unusual shape of this pot and the decorative openwork make it highly desirable and valuable, worth far more than a typical mustard pot because the chance to buy so seldom occurs. It was made in 1774 by William Vincent, a silversmith renowned for his good-quality openwork on tea caddies and other small wares.

This is a more typical example of the 1780s. Piercing as seen here, and open work as seen on the example above, should always be

checked carefully for damage. Other areas of potential weakness that should be examined carefully are:
*the hinge – may have been weakened
*the handle – can pull away from body
*the body – fragile because areas have been cut away and therefore vulnerable to damage.

During the reign of George IV highly elaborate decoration was favoured. On this typical example nearly all the surface is ornamented with blooms and scrolls.
*Pots with feet should be checked to make sure they have not been pushed up into the body. Feet are usually hollow and can wear through on their underside or become flattened through continual use.

Small, drum-shaped mustard pots were made from the 1820s onwards. This early Victorian example (c.1840) can be dated from the distinctive design around the base, reminiscent of the "melon" pattern also seen on teapots and entrée dishes produced at this time.

Beware

Some mustard pots have been converted from egg-cups or salt cellars and these are far less desirable. Ovoid pots, or those on three feet, should be avoided as should any pot that does not have cover marks.

FLATWARE (BEFORE 1750)

A set of twelve William III dog-nose pattern table forks; Isaac Davenport; 1701; value code B (the set)

Identification checklist for a set of dog-nose pattern table forks
1. Do the forks have three prongs?
2. Is there no sign of the fork having been made from a spoon?
3. Is there an original crest or coat-of-arms?
4. Is each fork marked at the bottom of the stem?
5. Are the marks identical and in exactly the same place? (Be suspicious if they are.)

Early flatware (before 1750)
Spoons are the earliest type of flatware to have been made, dating from the Roman times. Probably the most collectable early examples are Apostle spoons. By the 1680s the bowl of the spoon had changed from the earlier deep bowl to the shape it is today and had a "trefid" end. This became less pronounced until it matured into the "dog-nose" of the Queen Anne period.

Forks
Initially food was eaten with a spoon. Forks, a Continental invention, were not introduced into Britain until the Restoration, when they followed the styles of spoons. Early forks are far rarer and more desirable than spoons. The earliest forks have two or three prongs. Four prongs were introduced in the 1720s, but the two styles overlapped for a while. Three-pronged forks such as those in the main picture are highly sought-after today.
*Knives are not very practical and apart from very early ones which are interesting in their own right, are best avoided.
*Early spoons and forks usually

have a coat-of-arms; by the reign of George II a crest is more likely. Early examples are engraved on the back as they were put on the table "upside down".

Trefid spoons followed on from Apostle spoons (see pp. 164-165) and are very rare. The example pictured above left dates from c.1690 and is typically beautifully engraved, with winged putti and birds set amongst scrolling foliage. The pointed trefid end later flattened out into the dognose shape of the fork in the main picture. Value depends upon the quality of the engraving and state of wear.

The Hanoverian pattern superceded the dog-nose pattern, and was popular during the reign of George II. Hanoverian forks were made with either four prongs, or the more desirable three prongs illustrated here. This set of spoons and forks has been engraved with the arms of George Booth, 2nd Earl of Warrington, which makes them instantly very desirable and assures their high quality.

Marks
Many pieces from the 1730s onwards, have the metal folded over the marks where the silversmith has had to restore the shape of the stem after it had been flattened by the stamp. This was no doubt a factor in moving the marks to the top of the handle in the 1770s.

Early 18thC table knives such as these had rounded cannon handles, but by the mid 18thC they changed to the flatter pistol handles which were more comfortable to hold. These knives are very impractical as the steel blades need polishing each time they are used. Surprisingly, they seem to have survived in quantity and in sets. Cannon knives are much rarer than the later pistol variety and are worth many times as much.
*Ideally, the handle should have a maker's mark and the lion passant but often the marks are completely worn.

Condition
The steel blades of knives are often worn or rusty. In the example above they have been replaced (impossible to do today), which is not detrimental to the value. Knife handles are loaded and frequently the loading expands when the knife is put into water and the handle splits and cannot be repaired.

Makers
Flatware was made by specialist makers including Elias Cachart, Isaac Callard, Richard Crossley, and Eley, Fearn and Chawner.

FLATWARE (1750 ONWARDS)

An 18-place Regency table service; Paul Storr, London; 1813; value code A

Identification checklist for a late 18th/19thC service
1. Is there little variation from a "straight" set?
2. Is the set relatively free from wear?
3. If the forks are perfect, do they look as though they are the appropriate length?
4. Is each fork equally worn?
5. Are all the pieces of the same pattern?
6. Do any crests appear original?

Flatware services
From c.1780 flatware was increasingly made in services and there are many examples around to satisfy the high demand. Patterns became more elaborate and Victorian flatware is infinitely varied, particularly that made in the United States. Unlike very early forks and spoons, services are bought primarily for daily use.
*Up until the end of the 18thC flatware did not come in fitted boxes (with the exception of very elaborate dessert services which usually did).

Condition
Forks are often badly worn and some have been trimmed to "remove" the wear, but the prongs on these examples will be significantly shorter. It is not uncommon in boxed sets to find an unequal distribution of wear among the forks or spoons, as a set for 12 people, for example, may have been used by a household of six, leaving much of the set unused – these are best avoided.

Collecting
When buying a service of flatware it is most desirable to have the nearest combination to a "straight" set possible (all pieces made at the same time, by the same maker, with the same crests). However, one or two pieces in a set have often been replaced. Knives are rarely included and it is advisable to buy modern equivalents (a little

more difficult for earlier patterns which are no longer reproduced). Additional spoons and forks can be bought in any numbers; sets of six or 12 are the accepted quantities. Prices rise considerably for a "straight" set and for those in very good condition.

The feather edging on this set should be checked carefully to see how old it is, as this type of decoration was often added later.

to plain Old English services to add value. In this particular set the forks and knives are modern replacements; the rest were made in the 1770s. The stamped cartouche around the crest is very unusual.

Fiddle Thread and Shell are the most sought-after patterns. It is essential to look at all the items in a set because there is very little difference between some patterns (ie. between King's pattern and Queen's, see p. 64) and to the uninitiated eye they may seem the same.

Dessert services

Dessert services were made from c.1760. These are generally gilded and very elaborate and were made for the wealthy. The blade of this knife is typically 19thC in design. Dessert services are usually made of a heavy gauge metal and tend to be in good condition with the gilding intact.

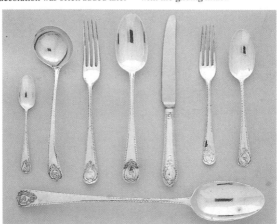

Basting spoons

By the end of the 18thC serving spoons and basting spoons were often included in services, but in the early part of the century they were made on their own.

Early basting spoons have exceptionally long cannon handles and a very deep bowl; this

Queen Anne basting spoon by William Mathew, 1704, is 18in (45¾cm) long. Such early spoons are rare and highly sought-after, and will command a high price even if they show signs of wear. Later serving spoons in services are not as interesting and are worth considerably less.

FLATWARE – BASICS

Patterns
The most popular patterns in flatware are King's, Fiddle Thread and Shell. The least popular is probably Fiddle, which is very plain. In general the most highly collected patterns are those for which it is easy to find matching pieces. If you were to buy a Victorian pattern such as Albert or Charlotte, or one from the 1930s, it would be far more difficult to find replacements than for the patterns established by the reign of George IV. The patterns most frequently encountered are Old English and Fiddle. Some may all look the same, but if put together variations are clear. Patterns which are still made today include King's, Old English and Rat Tail.
*Because flatware is so abundant any pieces that are worn should be avoided.
*Sets of cutlery are often sold in fitted cases, but very rarely do the bowls and handles fit properly into the canteen unless the case is original.

Spoon types
Illustrated below are a number of the most popular spoon designs.

Rat-tail
Produced in services from the mid-18thC onwards, although some earlier sets of spoons do exist.

Old English
Produced in services from the late 18thC onwards and still made today.

Onslow
An attractive and unusual design with a cast tip to the handle which is normally quite heavy. Developed in 1760 and made in sets subsequently, but rare.

Old English Thread
This design was mostly produced in the late 18thC.

Fiddle Thread.
This pattern was produced for a long time on the Continent before being made in Britain from the beginning of the 19thC. Fiddle pattern is the the same but without the "border". Much Scottish provincial silver is plain Fiddle, easily distinguished from the English by the longer terminal. The Scottish minor guilds are avidly collected and high prices are paid for rarities.

Hour Glass
This pattern was produced in quantity from the Regency period onwards.

King's
This popular pattern was produced from the Regency period onwards.

King's Husk
A pattern found on flatware produced from the Regency period onwards.

Queen's
A similar design to the King's pattern produced from the Regency period onwards.

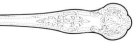

Albert or Charlotte
A popular pattern on flatware produced throughout the Victorian period.

Beaded
A pattern found mainly on flatware made in the Victorian period.

Albany
Another design found mainly on flatware produced during the Victorian period.

Scottish patterns
In Scotland the most elaborate designs – King's and Queen's – are sometimes struck on one side only in order to save money. These were less expensive when new and are relatively inexpensive now. They are also difficult to match today.

Collecting
A number of people, both trade and private, collect good pieces of any particular pattern in order to make up complete sets which are worth far more than individual items. Output of flatware was so vast that this is not too difficult a task, but each item would have to be polished and different crests removed. Because complete sets are so highly sought-after collectors will pay very high prices for them.
*Never match old patterns with those made recently as although they may look similar the quality is entirely different. Moreover, modern flatware is very expensive compared to the antique equivalent, so it is worth the search.

Wear
Worn flatware is one of the only types of silver not to be worth much more than the melt value of the metal, as satisfactory repair is almost impossible.

The spoon on the left is in good condition but the central one is worn – note how the bowl shape has been eroded. The spoon on the right has also suffered in usage, but has been reshaped to disguise wear. The bowl of this spoon, being thin from rework-ing, will be noticeably flexible; its unusual proportions should also arouse suspicion.

The fork on the left is in fairly good condition. The central one has been worn by years of scrap-ing across plates. The one on the right was similarly worn, but the tines have been trimmed level to disguise signs of wear. This is apparent when compared to an unaltered example, but can be difficult to spot otherwise.
*It is important to be satisfied with the feel of flatware; obvious-ly a sharp, worn bowl will not be comfortable in the mouth. Patina is relevant if buying a plain service. If buying anything other than a straight set do look at it closely. There are many small variations where there may or may not be spurs or scrolls at the base of the stem above the bowl, and where terminals on spoons may turn up or down.

DECORATIVE TABLEWARE

A pierced basket; c.1750

Among some of the more expensive items of silver available to the collector are the large decorative items which were bought by the rich largely as an external show of wealth. These are all very popular today because they can can used as attractive objects to display on a large table. Objects range from exuberant épergnes and centrepieces to large baskets, punch bowls and monteiths. Because these were mainly large and expensive items even when made, many of them were produced as presentation pieces and bear an inscription to this effect. Unfortunately, unless the inscription is particularly interesting, it will significantly lower the value of the piece.

Épergnes generally have a central basket and several smaller bowls. Early examples have candle sockets which are interchangeable with the smaller baskets. The first épergnes were made in the second quarter of the 18thC and their production coincided with the rise in popularity of the rococo style and the return to fashion of Chinese motifs first used in the 1680s. Épergnes were always highly decorative, and swirling naturalistic motifs and Chinese masks were applied with enthusiasm – there are even examples with pagoda roofs hung with bells.

Épergnes were replaced in the 19th century with the centrepiece, which at first was made to stand on its own in the centre of the table, but which later became the focal point of an entire decorative scheme of smaller pieces placed at intervals down the table. By the end of the century many centrepeices were made in Sheffield plate which made them more affordable. These examples are usually like the one illustrated on p. 145, which has smaller copies of the single figure holding the glass dish placed at either end of the centrepeice. Mirror plateaus – glass "trays" used to mirror the light – were seldom made at exactly the same time as the centrepiece, but they add greatly to the decorative effect and are an attractive addition. They are also sought-after on their own, particularly for displaying celebration cakes.

Silver baskets were first produced in the 1730s, and although early ones are rare those dating from the mid-18thC onwards are available in large numbers. Curiously, they seem to be almost exclusively a British idea, although some were produced in the United States. Most are pierced, and as they were in daily use for a long time it is important to check for damage. Particularly from the end of the 18thC baskets were made with simple wirework sides, or (on those in the more usual oval shape), wirework sides overlaid with sheafs of corn – both types are believed to have been for bread rather than fruit or cakes. Baskets tended to get lighter as the years progresed, probaly due to an increase in demand from the less wealthy section of the market. They also became shallower. Any baskets without handles should be checked carefully to make sure a handle has not been removed. A number of grand silver gilt examples were produced in the Regency period which are very expensive today. Baskets are popular with collectors as they can be used to display fruit attractively in the centre of a large table.

Punch bowls and monteiths both originated in the 1680s and were in general production for some 50 years or so. Monteiths were used for serving iced drinks. Unlike punch bowls they have handles, probably made necessary for carrying the bowls by the condensation that formed on the outside. Punch seems to have been mixed in the dining room and the bowl required a number of accessories. Most obvious is the ladle. This initally had a silver handle, but later it was wood, and then whale bone when it also became much smaller. Other acessories included orange strainers which had wide handles to go over the bowl but few of these have survived. Sugar was also a necessity in the punch-making process and the early sugar bowls without lids (see p. 113) were developed at this time.

Differences between porringers and caudle cups seem to be blurred, and both were designed to hold warm liquid. If caudle cups are defined as having baluster bodies (see p.81) their production was confined to the late 17thC. The porringer has a far longer life span and many of those seen today date from the 18thC. The American porringer is quite a different vessel to the British one and in England is rather improbably called a bleeding bowl (see p. 150 and p. 173).

A number of spout cups were produced as an alternative to the caudle cup. These are now very rare and seem to have been used for feeding the elderly and infirm.

ÉPERGNES

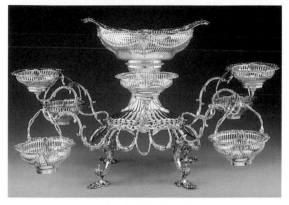

A George III nine basket épergne; Emick Rommer, London, 1772; ht 15in (38.1cm); value code B

Identification checklist for 18thC and 19thC épergnes
1. Are the body and central basket fully marked with the same set of marks?
2. Do all the other component parts (such as branches, baskets, swing handles) have some marks?
3. Is the piercing in good condition?
4. Are the swags or branches free from repairs? (If they have been snapped and soldered the piece is devalued.)
5. Are the feet undamaged?
6. Do any crests or coats-of-arms match on all the dishes? (Those with different crests are very suspect.)

Épergnes
Épergnes first appeared towards the middle of the 18thC. They were placed in the centre of grand dinner tables to hold fruit and sweetmeats. Most were originally supplied with wooden boxes to protect them when not in use. Rare and expensive, épergnes tend to get larger and wider as the century progresses; early ones from c.1730 are relatively compact. They have one central basket and a variable number of smaller ones; mid 18thC versions tend to have four side baskets and a larger central one. The épergne in the main picture has six side baskets, later in the 18thC the number could be even greater but in the 19thC fewer baskets returned to favour.

Marks
The body and central basket should have a full set of hall-marks. All the other parts should be part-marked, with the lion passant, maker's mark and, from 1784, the sovereign mark.

Condition
Because épergnes were grand pieces made for affluent households and used infrequently they tend to have survived in good condition. Épergnes should, however, always be carefully checked for damage especially on branches and feet. Branches were solid on earlier fine ones but later versions had loaded branches which are difficult to repair. The value of this one is reduced slightly because the branches are unmarked, indicating that they are possibly later replacements.
* Individual baskets which were once part of an épergne are often sold on their own, but as these do not have a full set of marks, their origin should be obvious.

The rare and early épergne below was made in Ireland c.1745 and like much Irish silver of the time lacks a date letter. Typically

for an early piece there are fewer baskets than later on. The Chinese figures on the main basket are seen on English cake or bread baskets of the period (see p. 72), and reflect the Irish fondness for the rococo style.

Decoration
The styles and decoration of épergnes reflects contemporary styles and fashions in other types of silver and applied arts of the period. Note how the early Irish example on the left has a strong, curvilinear form and incorporates typically lavish and varied rococo decoration, such as eagles, and Chinamen as well as the more usual flowers and scrolls; while the late 18thC épergne below uses a simple shape adorned by a restrained decorative border of anthemia and Vitruvian scrolls typical of the neo-classical period.

Glass liners
Glass liners – as seen on the épergne below made by William Pitts in London in 1786/7 – were a necessary addition to épergnes from the third quarter of the 18thC. The attractive blue colour of the glass was revealed by the openwork baskets. Épergnes are weighed without their liners.

Regency épergnes
Heavy florid shapes, with large low feet became fashionable in the early years of the 19thC. This characteristic Regency-style épergne was made by Matthew Boulton in Birmingham in 1819. The silver branches support shallow cut glass bowls.
*Damage to the glass bowls, or the replacement of bowls on Regency épergnes will reduce the value dramatically. But in fact Regency glass is in some ways easier to replace than Victorian glass. Victorian glass is frequently frosted and engraved

and this is virtually impossible to match up satisfactorily with existing glass today – copying a cut glass bowl is far easier.

69

CENTREPIECES

An early Victorian centrepiece; Richard Sawyer; Dublin; 1843; ht 25in (64cm); value code B

Identification checklist for a Victorian centrepiece
1. Is it marked on every detachable part (ie. body, figures, sconces, branches, base etc.)?
2. Is each individual branch numbered or marked with identical dots?
3. Are all parts of the decoration intact?
4. If there is a mirror plateau, is it silver? (It could be electroplate.)
5. If the mirror plateau is not silver, does it match the centrepiece?

Centrepieces
The épergne was replaced by the centrepiece in the late 18thC. They were made both with and without candlesticks and had a central bowl for holding fruit. They tend to have fewer side bowls than épergnes. The bowl

was either solid silver or pierced, in which case it had a glass liner. The liners are often missing, and because they were usually frosted and engraved, they are hard to copy today. They can add considerably to the decorative effect of a centrepiece and an obvious replacement will lower the value.

Mirror plateaus
The centrepiece in the main picture is a typical Victorian example. It comes complete with a mirror plateau. These can easily become separated from the body and can be sold on their own – they are particularly popular with the catering profession who use them display wedding cakes.

Care
Centrepieces are virtually impossible to clean properly on a regular basis. It is advisable to have them professionally cleaned and then covered with a protecting surface which will prevent them from tarnishing. It is best to then to handle them only with protective gloves.

Centrepieces from the 1820s were relatively simple in design. The ladies supporting the bowls on their heads on this example were a common subject – check that they would not have been holding anything in their hands. Also make sure the base, figures and top bowl match, as the parts can get separated – sometimes the figures are mounted on wooden plinths and sold individually.
*This centrepiece has been considerably devalued by a lengthy inscription, added over 130 years later. It is too lengthy to contemplate successful removal.

This George III centrepiece made by Benjamin Smith in 1814 is of the first style to emerge and it has obvious similarities with épergnes (see pp. 68-69). The mirror plateau was made nine years later (the decoration on the band does not correspond to that on the dish), but this will not significantly devalue the piece. The winged paw feet on the plateau were very popular at this time.
*On this centrepiece it would be possible to match up the glass dishes as they are neither acid-etched nor frosted.
*Centrepieces came in fitted wooden boxes with baize-lined compartments for the arms but often kept in dark and damp cellars very few have survived the passage of time.

By the second half of the 19thC centrepieces were often reduced to one central basket on a stand without any fitments for candles – this one made by Elkington & Co. of Birmingham in 1861 is a typical example. Centrepieces became increasingly shorter and soon developed into dessert stands which replaced centrepieces at the end of the century.

BASKETS 1

*A George II silver Chinoiserie cake basket; S Herbert & Co.;
1756; lgth 13¾in (34.6cm); value code B*

Identification checklist for an 18thC basket
1. Is the basket marked on the top in the piercing or
underneath in a straight line?
2. Is the handle part marked to match?
3. If there is still a coat-of-arms present in the base of
the basket does it conform in style to the date of the
basket?
4. Is any bright-cut or pierced decoration in good
condition?
5. Has the handle remained intact?

Baskets
Baskets became fashionable from
c.1730 onwards and were placed
in the centre of a table to hold
fruit, bread, cakes or sweetmeats.
Although they were relatively
expensive items they were
produced in surprisingly large
numbers. They are highly decorative and still command a premium today.

Styles and shapes vary, but up
until the end of the 18thC most
had some form of pierced decoration which can be vulnerable to
damage and should be carefully
examined. Baskets often stand on
a rimmed foot; others have

separate bases and these should
be fully-marked, with part marks
on the body and handle.

The mid-18thC fashion for
chinoiserie motifs is reflected in
the Chinamen busts and
moustachioed mandarins with
which the basket in the main
picture is decorated. This
particular basket was made in
London in 1756 by S. Herbert &
Co., a company renowned for this
type of decoration.
*Chinoiserie decoration is
particularly sought-after. It is not
very common on baskets and
adds about 50 per cent to
their value.

Three desirable features add to the value of this basket which was made by Edward Aldridge of London in 1746:
*attractively shaped and decorated handle
*masks of Ceres heading the feet
*a good weight – 57oz (114dwt). By this time baskets were becoming shallower.

The most commonly-seen baskets are those dating from the late 18thC, of oval-shape with swing handle and pierced decora-tion. Like many baskets this one is not very heavy, weighing 29oz (58dwt). The attractive bright-cut decoration adds to its desirability, as does the fact that it was made by the well-known silversmith Hester Bateman.

Marks
18thC baskets may be marked in a line on one of the straight lines of the piercing. Handles should also be marked to correspond with those on the body.

Condition
The intricate pierced decoration on the basket on the left needs careful checking for damage or signs of previous repairs. On many baskets the rim has been folded over by having excess weight placed on top. Any basket which stands on four feet should be checked, as the feet are easily pushed up through the body and are also prone to cracking. In the following decade baskets with a pierced apron support (see below) became popular. These too are vulnerable to damage.

This relatively light-weight basket, made in London in 1773, exemplifies the less lavish pieces made in the 1770s; it weighs only 20oz (280g), only half as much as the one illustrated on the left. The pierced body and entwined handle are also of a very much simpler form than the earlier examples illustrated and the basket is worth significantly less as a result.

BASKETS 2 (AFTER c.1780)

*A George IV silver basket; Kirkby, Waterhouse & Co., Sheffield;
1820; lgth 13½in (34cm); value code D*

Identification checklist for a 19thC basket
1. Is the decoration chased rather than pierced?
2. Does the decoration correspond to that on salvers of
the time?
3. Does the decoration feature flowers, shells, foliage
and S-scrolls?
3. Is the basket relatively heavy?
4. Are all the separate pieces marked?
5. Is the handle free from damage?

Late 18thC and 19thC baskets
Chased decoration featuring
flowers, shells, foliage and S-
scrolls was popular on baskets
made during the reign of George
IV and followed the decoration
on salvers of the day. This type of
basket with an unpierced body
remained popular until the end of
the 19thC.

Provincial baskets
London makers tend to
command a premium, so the
value of the basket in the main
picture, although of good quality,
will be lower than a London-
made example. Few baskets were
marked outside London at this
time as many provincial makers
sent them to the capital for assay.

Despite its slightly unusual open
lattice body, this 1785 Wakelin &
Taylor basket is deceptively
heavy, weighing 44oz (188dwt).

Baskets of this design were also made without a handle, some by Paul Storr.

Beware
A removed handle may be difficult to detect, but if there is a scratchweight this can be checked against the present weight of the basket – a significant loss in weight may mean a handle (or a coat-of-arms) has been removed.

The wide, broad rim and shallow shape of this basket, made by James Charles Edington of London in 1839, allow maximum surface area for the elaborate rococo-style adornments favoured in the Victorian period. The body weight of unpierced baskets often puts excessive strain on their relatively fragile handles and many have broken at some stage or been damaged so they refuse to sit properly. Always check carefully for any damage.
*Baskets of this type always had a handle and are not collectable if it has been removed.

Value
Silver of the later Victorian period is readily available and is usually far less expensive than silver produced in the 18thC or early 19thC. The basket illustrated above would only be worth about half as much as the one in the main picture which, although of a similar style and made in Sheffield rather than in London, was made 20 years earlier.

This shell-shaped basket with mermaid handle and dolphin feet is one of the most unusual and desirable basket styles. It was made by Edward Farrell in 1839, but the design is a copy of baskets first made in the 1740s. Baskets of this type are particularly susceptible to three types of damage:
*cast feet pushed up through the partially pierced body
*tears to the body caused by lifting with the handle
*wear to the ribs which will be thin.
Early baskets, including the original of the example above, tend to be far heavier than later reproductions due to the absence of a light touch in the piercing. Some supremely elegant pierced baskets were made as early as the 1760s and some very dull ones were made without any pierced decoration in the 1790s.

Late Victorian baskets
Typical of baskets of the late Victorian period is this pair made by C. S. Harris at the turn of the century. They were often made in sets of two or more and came in a wide variety of sizes. Most are of good quality and they remain highly sought-after by collectors. Value is affected by size: pairs or sets of larger sizes are especially desirable. This type of basket is frequently found in silver gilt which again enhances the price if it has remained in good condition.

PUNCH BOWLS

A punch bowl; Louis Mettayer;
1718; 8½in (21.5cm) diam., 25oz (50dwt); value code B

Identification checklist for an 18thC punch bowl
1. Is the bowl marked in a group underneath?
2. Is there a large contemporary coat-of-arms? (A plain surface, or anything small, such as a crest, would be suspect.)
3. Does the bowl have an elaborate cartouche? Are the arms contemporary with the cartouche?
4. Has it been left relatively unpolished so that the attractive patina has not been removed?
5. Is there no evidence of any engraving having been removed?
6. Is there a absence of splits around the rim?

Punch bowls
Unlike monteiths (see pp. 78 79) punch bowls do not have a scalloped, detachable rim, and they tend to be deeper. The earliest ones date from the last quarter of the 17thC when punch, a drink made from claret, brandy and spices, was introduced to Britain from India. After c.1730, glass replaced silver, and any silver punch bowls after this date tend to have been made as prizes, or as reproductions.

Collecting
Early punch bowls are very expensive, and today are bought primarily for decorative purposes, as a centrepiece, rather than for use. Appearances at auction are infrequent as they were not made in large quantities because of their size. Occasionally, monteiths without their rims are sold as punch bowls but this is usually apparent because a monteith has a plain wire rim on which the collar sits and a punch bowl does not. None of the bowls illustrated has a handle, which must have made them very awkward to move when full. Perhaps this confirms that punch was made and distributed in one place, the dining room, whereas a monteith was filled with ice and water and carried about to wherever the drink was to be poured. Constantly moving a monteith about would also account for so many missing collars.

Bowls became gradually broader and shallower with a taller rim. This example made by Gabriel Sleath in 1727 is particularly desirable as it has a fine contemporary inscription and engraving of a sailing ship. It is larger than the one in the main picture – 9½in (24cm) diam. – and significantly heavier – 45oz (90dwt).
*Although British engravers executed some wonderful designs, they never signed their work, whereas Continental engravers and some Americans did.

Marks
Early bowls are usually marked in a straight line along the side. Most 18thC examples are marked underneath in the points of a compass. Later bowls are marked on the side again. Marks underneath should be safe, but marks on the side of a large plain surface may be rubbed away by over zealous cleaning. If marked underneath make sure the marks have not been let in.

Many later bowls were made as presentation prizes. This example by Hester Bateman, 1789, is one of a series of punch bowls made for race prizes at Chester. The feet on punch bowls at this time have become taller. Because the surface is so plain the patina is very important; collectors will not buy one that has been over-polished.

Condition
Check the rims of bowls carefully for splits or repairs. Also look for damage where the foot joins the body.

Armorials and cartouches
As with any large plain surface check that a previous crest or coat-of-arms has not been removed and replaced with a later one – in particular, check carefully vacant cartouches like the one on the bowl on the left as it is very unlikely that a piece of silver of this size would have been left anonymous.
*There is always a slight possibility with a cartouche that has been chased in high relief that it can disguise the insertion of an engraved disc which has been paced over the top of the original coat-of-arms. This can be difficult to detect if the style of the cartouche is correct for the style of the punch bowl.

Punch bowls became progressively larger over the years and were made in even smaller quantities than previously; this example made by Smith and Sharp in 1761 is 12in (30cm) in diameter, and very heavy – 66oz (132dwt). The shell and scroll border of the cartouche is in keeping with the borders on salvers of the Regency period.

Decoration
The bowl above has been attractively decorated with elaborate chasing of bunches of grapes in bands around the top and base, which is typical of the Georgian period and reflects the use of the bowl as a vessel for holding alcohol. If the decoration were Victorian, it would be much more repetitive and cover the whole area.

77

MONTEITHS

*A Queen Anne monteith; Nathaniel Lock;
1704; 7½ in (19cm) high, 51oz (102dwt); value code A*

Identification checklist for an 18thC monteith
1. Is it fully marked on the side?
2. Does the collar bear corresponding marks?
3. Does it have side handles? (Punch bowls do not generally have handles.)
4. Does the bottom border on the collar match the top rim of the bowl?
5. Is there a contemporary coat-of-arms?
6. Are the foot of the bowl, and the handles, free from damage, and are the tops of the scrolls on the collar free from splits?

Monteiths

Monteiths are said to have got their name from a Scotsman called Monteith who reputedly wore a cloak with a scalloped edge. Monteiths are distinguishable from punch bowls by their wavy borders and side handles. On later examples the rim became detachable for practical purposes, so that the bowl could also be used for punch, and on many examples that come up for sale today, the collar is missing. The first monteiths appeared in 1683 and they continued to be produced up until the 1730s. They were used for keeping glasses cool; they would be filled with iced water in which the glasses would sit, held from their stems from the notches in the rim. Monteiths became larger over the years and by the 1690s had acquired handles, usually hung from lion's masks.
*Like punch bowls, monteiths are rare and expensive; those by the important makers of the period are particularly sought-after.

Damage

The collars of monteiths were frequently removed and because they are rather flimsy in structure they often needed some coaxing to fit into the bowl, and therefore are quite prone to damage. In particular, check carefully for splits around the decoration and repairs to the cherubs' heads. In addition the marks are sometimes well-rubbed.

Although this monteith by John Read dates from the same year as the one in the main picture (1704) the style is a little earlier, with a fluted body which is not only decorative, but which adds strength to the item. The handles are simpler than on the previous example and there is a good contemporary coat-of-arms. The scroll and cherub head decoration is typical of the period. This photograph illustrates clearly the construction of the monteith with a detachable collar.

*The coat-of-arms on the monteith in the main picture is earlier than the piece itself which suggests the engraver was copying from an older piece of silver. This is an attractive quirk, but if the piece bears a later coat-of-arms it suggests the original arms have been removed and this is undesirable.

Irish monteiths are very rare. This example from 1715 by the well-known maker, David King, is particularly solid and weighs (63oz, 126dwt). Although the collar is decorated with the scroll-work of previous examples, the masks and shells have disappeared.

Beware
A large plain surface such as that on the bowl above should be checked carefully for removal of arms; if any engraving has been removed the inside of the bowl will have a dip and be quite thin.

Marks
Both the bowl of the monteith and the detachable collar should be fully marked, in a line.

This monteith made by William Gamble in 1720 is probably one of the latest examples to be found. It is robust and plain and now has no handles (possibly because monteiths were no longer used for cooling glasses). As with later bowls, this monteith was awarded as a prize, this time at Northallerton races in 1722. The engraving makes it more interesting to the collector, especially one with an interest in racing.

*Many drinking items were presented as race prizes in the 18thC. These include beakers, tumbler cups and punch bowls as well as monteiths.

Reproductions
Reproductions of monteiths were made at the end of the 19thC and beginning of the 20thC, as an alterntive to rose bowls, when an upsurge in wealth increased demand for such items.

PORRINGERS AND CAUDLE CUPS

An 18thC porringer;
1739; ht 7in (18cm); value code E

Identification checklist for an 18th century porringer
1. Is there a band of lobing around the base?
2. Is there a corded girdle?
3. Are the handles flat strap if later, or cast if early?
4. Does it have a late-17thC-style cartouche?
5. Is the body gently flared?
6. Is it marked underneath in a group or on the side?
7. Is the decoration embossed? (Usually with acanthus or palm leaves.)

Porringers
Porringers are two-handled cylindrical cups, originally for porridge or gruel. They were made in quite large numbers from the mid-17thC right through to the middle of the 18thC.

Caudle cups
Caudle cups, although very similar to porringers, tend to have a baluster body, and were made for only a short period of around 50 years in the second half of the 17thC. Caudle was a sweet mixture of wine and milk which was given to invalids and women in childbirth, and quite often the cups were made as presentation gifts to mothers. Because the liquid might be given to invalids a few were made with a spout (see opposite).
*The earliest porringers and caudle cups tend to have lids; later ones do not.

One of the earliest porringers is this Charles II example made in 1680 by John Sutton. Typically, the decoration is chased and rather restrained, featuring an embossed band of palm and acanthus leaves. The handles are cast and are characteristically quite plain, in the shape of scrolls.
*Check the undecorated areas carefully to make sure a crest or coat-of-arms has not been removed.

This porringer from 1690 is typical of early examples, which had a base that resembled a rimmed foot. The handles are always cast, but here they are particularly elaborate; they could equally well have been plain (see previous example). The contemporary coat-of-arms are those of a widow, as they appear within a lozenge. The embossed decoration of acanthus leaves in particular can be found on contemporary tankards (see p. 87).

Condition
Check for holes in the chasing and any solder repairs in the decoration. Look carefully at the handles for breaks. Because the handles are susceptible to straining they may have been pulled away from the body. In addition, porringers which sit directly on their bases are prone to damage as the metal underneath is sometimes thin. This type of damage has usually been repaired in the past with soft solder.

Marks
Caudle cups and porringers are marked on the base in a group, or on the body near the lip by the handle in a straight line.
*Some porringers and caudle cups were made with covers (including the caudle cup illustrated below) and these should also be marked with a full set of hallmarks.

The baluster shape of this cup from 1672 suggests it is a caudle cup. The embossed and punched decoration is typical of the period; the chasing is not in high relief and is quite coarse and the background is matted. The condition of matting is a good indication of wear; if it is over-polished it will be almost shiny and should be avoided. The family's initials are visible beneath the rim. Although quite small (3in (8cm) high) caudle cups tend to be expensive as they were made for only a short period and are now very rare.

Spout cups
Spout cups were made for a very short period at the end of the 17thC as an alternative to the caudle cup and are very rare today. The spouts make the cups look so incongruous that they were frequently assumed to be fakes. Early examples were of a straight sided tankard shape with a curved spout; later pieces such as the one below were much more like porringers.

Marks
Spout cups were always made with a cover which is marked, like the lid of a tankard, in a straight line across the top, but sometimes these lids are missing.

This Queen Anne spout cup was made in 1702 by William Andrews. It has some particularly unattractive solder around the spout which could possibly add even more doubt to its authenticity. Spout cups were usually left plain, although a number were engraved with a crest or coat-of-arms.

DRINKING VESSELS

A silver-gilt wine goblet, c.1815

A huge amount of drinking vessels – cups, tankards, goblets and jugs – have been made over the centuries; and they are very popular with collectors today. Most of those that have survived date from the 18thC onwards. Because they were generally very well-used condition is an important consideration – in particular check any handles for straining, and the rims for splits.

In Britain beakers were produced on a large scale for domestic use. Most are very simple in design as befits such a utilitarian object. The exceptions are those beakers made for travelling grandees, produced predominantly on the Continent, which came in sets together with a knife, fork, spoon and spice box, assembled in a small silver case. These are always of very high quality with intricate engraving, and are highly sought-after. In the United States beakers with a pronounced Dutch influence in height and decoration were made in New York in the late 17thC. However, any later examples seem to have primarily been destined for Church, rather than domestic use.

Tumbler cups, mostly broad and shallow, have always been popular with collectors because they are small, attractive and very tactile. The first ones were made in the 17thC and they continued to be produced throughout the 18thC.

However, they are rare and consequently prices are always high. Many later tumbler cups were engraved and presented as race prizes.

Tankards were made in huge numbers both in England and the United States, although less were produced in Scotland and Ireland. They seem to have been immune to changes in fashion and nearly all have a plain body with the simple addition of either a band of chased acanthus leaves or Chinoiserie flat chasing at the base in the reign of Charles II, or a band of gadrooning at the end of the 17thC. It was not until the Regency period that tankards became ornate, and then massive examples were produced in silver gilt to be given as presentation pieces. The Victorians, who disliked any plain surfaces, often added elaborate chasing in the form of animals, leaves and scrolls to earlier vessels. These tankards used to be virtually impossible to sell, but there is now a modest market for them if they are suitably attractive. Tankards were frequently converted into more useful jugs during the 19thC but these tend to be less elegant than the original. To be legal the conversion must have later marks on any additions such as the spout. An interesting variation to the standard tankard is a design produced on the east coast of Britain, in York and to a lesser extent Newcastle. These show a Baltic influence and have pegs down the inside of the body to ensure fair shares for all at drinking parties.

The mug may seem a fairly obvious derivation of the tankard, but it did not appear in Britain until the late 17thC, and American examples were later still. Irish mugs are very rare. Like tankards, mugs were primarily plain until the end of the 18thC. In Victorian times small mugs were popular as gifts, especially at christenings, and they were made in a huge variety of styles with profuse decoration. Very many early plain mugs have been later decorated; others have been converted into small cream jugs by the addition of a lip, and as with most alterations these are likely to be illegal unless the additional parts have been hallmarked. As with most silver any deviation from the original object will cause a significant fall in the value.

Some of the most decorative drinking vessels are 18thC goblets. Bright-cut examples made in the 1790s, in particular, can command substantial prices if they are still in pristine condition. Unlike mugs, it would be difficult to decorate a goblet at a later date as most already have some form of engraving. Those produced throughout the Victorian era were particularly fancy, when they were sometimes made with matching jugs.

A later alternative to the tankard was the beer jug, produced in the 18thC. Beer jugs were expensive when new despite the fact that most of them were plain. More elaborate exceptions are early jugs with cut-card decoration around the spout and base, and some very elegant and restrained Neo-Classical jugs from the 1780s by such makers as Boulton and Fothergill. Victorian jugs had finer decoration on the body and were made for wine rather than beer.

BEAKERS AND TUMBLERS

A Charles II beaker; London;
1665; ht 3⅝in (9.2cm); value code D

Identification checklist for a Charles II beaker
1. Is it marked in a group underneath?
2. Does it have a separate reeded foot?
3. Is the cylindrical body slightly flared at the lip?
4. Is there a leafy band of chased or engraved decoration around the top of the beaker?
5. Is the rim free from splits?
6. Does it have an original crest or coat of-arms?

Beakers
The earliest beakers date from before English silver was hall-marked and are fairly common both in Britain and on the Continent, although rare in the United States. Early ones often had lids. After the Reformation beakers were occasionally used as communion cups and many true communion cups of the time have a beaker-shaped bowl. Form changes very little, although 16thC and early 17thC examples tend to be taller with a slightly broader base than later ones.

Decoration
Beakers are usually quite plain apart from a crest or coat-of-arms, although those dating from the reign of Charles II often have chased decoration of leaves and flowers. Beakers which were made as part of travelling sets are generally intricately engraved.

Tumbler cups
Tumbler cups are beaten from thick guage silver with most of the weight in the base so that the cups return to an upright position when put on their side. Because they are so solid they are almost impossible to damage. Most date from the late 17thC, but they were also made throughout the 18thC. Early ones tend to be short and very broad in relation to their height; later ones are taller and thinner. Most of them are plain, but because they are very tactile objects they are popular with collectors today.

Marks

Tumbler cups are usually marked in a group underneath the base or near the rim. Beakers were marked underneath the base until the end of the 18thC when they are marked in a line under the rim.

This William and Mary silver beaker made in London in 1693 is typically plain apart from the additon of the contemporary engraved initials near the rim.
*As with any piece of plain silver the surface should have a nice aged patina – any over-shiny beakers should be avoided as they may have been restored.

The beaker in this late 17thC travelling set is of a typically oval shape and is elaborately engraved with winged cherubs and scrolling flowers. The beaker is fitted with a wooden insert which holds three handles onto which can be screwed a knife, fork and spoon, and it also has a spice box. Complete sets such as this are very rare and sought-after. The value is increased because it is still in its original shagreen case.

*These sets are often unmarked. Parts of this example have a London hallmark for 1687 which has been struck over a German mark, which suggests the piece was originally made in Germany.

The broad shallow shape of this tumbler cup from 1698 is typical of the period. Crests or coats-of-arms are engraved on more expensive ones, but frequently the surface is plain or bears just the initials of the owner. Because the cups are often marked underneath, the marks tend to be well-worn. Those with very faint marks should be avoided as many better examples can be found.

By the 1750s tumbler cups were far narrower in relation to their height. This one has an attractive coat-of-arms and is one of a pair, which increases its value.
*Occasionally beakers and tumbler cups were made in nesting sets, when the cups fit inside each other; these have long-since been split up and are rarely complete today. Beakers and cups were made in pairs in the 18thC, but few are found as such today.
*Many surviving beakers and tumbler cups were made in provincial towns such as Newcastle and York.

EARLY TANKARDS
(PRE c.1765)

A silver tankard; William Shaw, London; 1764; ht 7½in (19cm); value code D

Identification checklist for a mid-18th-century English tankard

1. Does the tankard have a baluster-shaped body?
2. Is the lid domed?
3. Is the upper body marked in a line near the side of the handle or in a group underneath?
4. Does the inside of the lid have identical marks to those on the body, in a group?
5. Is the body quite plain, possibly with only a girdle for ornament?
6. Does the tankard have a rimmed foot?
7. Has the handle been hammered from sheet metal rather than cast?

Tankards

Tankards made from silver provided a popular and more robust alternative to drinking vessels made from stoneware. Although pieces dating from the reign of Charles I and the Commonwealth period have survived, the vast majority date from the end of the 17thC or later, probably because earlier pieces were melted down during the Civil War. Silver tankards were made for private domestic use; throughout the 17th century they were prohibited by law from being used in public houses. Initially introduced for holding ale (a sweet sticky mead, quite unlike the beer of today), tankards were made in in relatively large numbers. They remain among the most readily available pieces of 17thC silver, and continued to be used as drinking vessels until the late-18thC. The mid-18thC example illustrated in the main picture is of average quality and shows the simple baluster-shape and domed lid which was popular at the time.

Marks

Tankards of the 17thC usually have four marks placed in a straight line by the handle; the same marks were also stamped on the lid (usually on the top near the handle). By the early 18thC marks on the lid were more usually found inside the vessel. Unlike other lidded tablewares, tankards with a full set of marks on the body should be expected to have the same marks on the lid – those which do not are almost certainly "wrong".

Plain shapes and simple decorative borders are characteristic of early tankards such as this straight-sided version made in 1663. Apart from a coat-of-arms the tankard is decorated only by a trimmed wire foot and an interesting thumbpiece.

Lids

Early tankards had simply-stepped lids as seen in the example above. Later, shallow domes, progressing to more pronounced domes, were favoured. Lids are occasionally subject to alteration; stretched marks on a domed lid may indicate that it was once flat. In the late 17thC tankards often had a peak to the lid which did not survive for long. Thumb pieces range from volute or corkscrew on early examples to openwork on later tankards.

Armorials

Tankards were important and expensive purchases and were recognized as being a tangible symbol of their owner's wealth; not surprisingly most were there-fore marked with their owner's arms or initials. If the coat-of-arms on the side of a tankard is contemporary with the piece it will add significant value and interest to the tankard. If the arms have been erased (see p. 15) the value would be reduced by at least a third.

The chased acanthus leaves and foliage on this London tankard from 1680 are the only decoration usually seen on English tankards until the Regency period. *Marks sometimes move to accommodate decoration. On this example the marks on the lid are unusually close to the front because the lid is decorated near to the handle.

This early-18thC tankard with its baluster body and modest-domed lid shows how the form has evolved from the straight sided examples with flat-topped lids of the previous decades.

Condition

The area around the handle socket is particularly vulnerable to wear and should be checked for damage or signs of weakness. Perhaps more than any other item of silver, tankards have had changes to coats-of-arms. Always check carefully for thinness.

LATER TANKARDS
(POST c.1765)

A silver tankard; John Langland, Newcastle; 1802; ht 7½in (19cm); value code D

Identification checklist for a tankard c.1780-c.1800
1. Does it have a sheet handle?
2. Is the lid flat rather than domed?
3. Is the only decoration in the form of applied bands around the body?
4. Is there a coat-of-arms? (A desirable feature.)
5. Is the body straight-sided and of cylindrical shape?
6. Is there any damage to the handle joints?
7. Is any gilding in good condition?

Later tankards
By the end of the 18thC the use of tankards as drinking vessels had declined, largely because ale-drinking had been replaced by wine-drinking in fashionable circles. The tankard in the main picture is typical of those made during the final period of production before reproductions were made. Similar examples were also made in fused plate. Tankards continued to be made after this into the Regency and Victorian periods, but these were produced in far smaller numbers and were made primarily as decorative or presentation pieces. Most of them are highly elaborate but shapes copy earlier styles.

Decoration
Motifs taken from classical antiquity, such as bacchanalia and pastoral scenes, typify the more elaborate decoration on early 19thC tankards. Silver gilt was popular on Regency silver (see opposite) but check the decoration underneath is not worn as this means that the gilding has been added at a later date

Regency tankards were produced primarily as presentation gifts, and they are usually large, heavy and lavishly decorated. This silver gilt example, which was made by Storey and Eliot in 1812, is typically elaborate. The classical motifs of drinking cherubs have been cast and applied which makes it significantly heavier than earlier tankards – this one weighs two or three times more than any of the tankards illustrated on the previous pages.
*Regency tankards are considerably more expensive than earlier ones. This tankard is worth up to five times the value of a mid-18thC example.

Although this tankard was made by John Langland in Newcastle in 1769, it is a direct copy of a Scandinavian design. Trade routes between the east coast of Britain and Germany and the Baltic states were well established by the 17thC, and many examples of tankards on three ball feet were imported during this time. Copies of continental tankards were made in York, and to a lesser extent in Newcastle,

and were marked with the usual English marks. Very few examples were made in London.

Pegs
Some Continental tankards (and British copies) had pegs spaced down the inside wall of the tankard which served as markers for drinkers. According to tradition these gave rise to the popular saying, to "take someone down a peg or two".

Beware
With any ball-footed silver items the state of the balls is of paramount importance since they are made from hollow metal and frequent use can cause splitting. Spherical ball feet also tend to flatten with use and on some tankards they may have been removed, turned round and reapplied; others may have replacement feet.
*The applied foliage at the feet of the tankard below left will greatly strengthen it.

During the Victorian period over-embellishment reached a peak and many earlier silver items were profusely chased to make them more attractive to Victorian taste. Although this tankard was made in 1711 it has been decorated at a later date with elaborate chasing of scrolls and flowers. Initially, it would have had a plain body apart from the original early 18thC coat-of-arms which is now barely visible through all the chasing.
*Although this type of alteration will usually diminish value it is only illegal if silver has been added to the original piece (see p. 10). This example is worth only around one fifth of the value of what it would have been if it had not been altered.

MUGS

A silver mug; Richard Gurney & Co., London; 1750; ht 4in (9.7cm); value code E

Identification checklist for an 18thC mug
1. Is the mug marked in a group underneath?
2. Are the marks in pristine condition?
3. Is the crest or coat-of-arms original?
4. Does the mug stand on a separate foot?
5. Is the handle cast?
6. Is the body baluster-shaped?
7. Are there no splits in the rim?
8. Are the reinforcing patches at the handles original rather than a later addition?
9. Is there no damage to the sockets where the handle joins the body?

Mugs
The earliest mugs likely to be encountered date from the end of the 17thC and have slightly tapering cylindrical sides on a flat base. Late 17thC mugs include the "thistle" shape which originated in Scotland, but was also made in England. At this date mugs have strap handles raised from sheet, and the bodies are generally plain, apart from a band of lobes and flutes, also found on late 17thC tankards. Other decoration such as chasing will almost certainly be an 18thC addition and is likely to include removal and replacement of the original arms or crest. The

baluster-shaped mug was established in 1715, and usually has a cast handle. This shape predominated until the 1770s when straight-sided mugs were made with sheet handles – a change perhaps assisted by the ready supply of sheet metal from the new rolling mills. Mugs, like tankards, ceased to be used for beer drinking in the late 18thC. Tankards are large and have lids; mugs are smaller and do not have lids and silversmiths found an alternative use for them as small presents. They were made for this purpose, mostly smaller than before, throughout the 19thC in a variety of styles.

The simple strap handle and banding on this rare, early mug from 1688 are typical of the period. The value of this example is significantly increased by the Chinoiserie decoration which is particularly unusual to find on a mug. However because there is fairly little Chinoiserie it is relatively inexpensive when compared to other pieces with similar decoration.

Irish mugs
The slightly tapering, straight sides of this Dublin mug from 1732 were a popular alternative to

the baluster shape of the mug in the main picture. However, the tucked-in foot would not appear on an English mug and is peculiar to Irish examples. Check the foot carefully for old splits and for any solder repairs.
*The coat-of-arms within the simple Baroque cartouche is that of a widow.
*Most mugs were made singly, but as with much silver, any made in pairs – as in this example – will be worth more than twice the value of one.

Christening mugs
Many later more highly-decorated mugs of the 19thC were made as christening presents, the finest of which came in cased sets with a knife, fork and spoon.

This christening set was made by G.W. Adams for Chawner & Co. in 1875. It is appropriately decorated with revelling cherubs and has a handle in the shape of a vine branch. This particular design was given by Queen Victoria to her godchildren on various occasions and any with an interesting inscription will command a premium.

This mug by Hunt and Roskell (1878) is charmingly decorated with figures representing the four seasons. The knife, fork and spoon were made by Francis Higgins, a well-known maker of elaborate flatware. The value of the set is greatly increased by the fact that it is still in its case.
*The mugs are usually of high quality and many have survived virtually unused. But the spoon has often been well-used and may be badly worn.

GOBLETS

*A late 18thC goblet;
c.1790; ht 6¼in (16cm); value code E*

Identification checklist for a late 18thC goblet
1. Is the goblet vase-shaped?
2. Does it have a stem foot?
3. Is there any engraved decoration?
4. Is the decoration bright-cut and in good, crisp condition ?
5. Is it fully marked, probably underneath the base or on the rim foot?

Goblets
Goblets, or wine cups, the distinction is sometimes blurred, which were made for secular use do not seem to pre-date Elizabethan times. It is easy to distinguish them from communion cups of the period which in general have beaker-shaped bowls, whereas 19thC goblets have bowls in almost any other style. With the event of the Civil War very little silver was made and when Charles II returned he brought with him continental fashions and new ideas. The novelty and availability of glass meant that silver cups for wine were forgotten about until reproductions were made in the 1770s. The onset of Neo-Classicism with its fondness for vase-shaped forms was entirely suited to the goblet which remained in this style until the Regency period.

Collecting
Most 18thC goblets are vase-shaped but the standard and extent of decoration can vary considerably and this will alter the price. Several features add to the desirability of the goblet above:
*high-quality bright cut engraving in perfect sparkling condition
*the addition of a fitted case which has protected the goblet
*gilding on the inside of the bowl
*fine original crest and initials.
It is interesting to see that the goblet is fitted with a retailer's label for Rundell, Bridge and Rundell as this demonstrates the range of makers working for this reputable company at this time.

This Charles I wine goblet relies on form alone for its appeal. A good patina is crucial to a good price. Unlike many types of plain silver, early goblets always seem to have been looked after and do not suffer from later decoration. They are often found without a crest. Because they are marked in a line below the rim the marks have sometimes been badly worn down. Decoration on goblets of this period includes chased blooms and strapwork.

Vase-shaped goblets were made in large quantities throughout the 18thC and 19thC, and value therefore largely depends on the quality of the decoration and the reputation of the maker. The best examples are in silver gilt and have bright-cut engraving and a good coat of arms; the most ordinary are plain and light-weight. This goblet, made as one

of a pair, is quite plain, but it is of high quality and is still in good condition.
*Goblets should be solid – any which can be squeezed should be avoided.
*Unlike mugs, which were made singly, goblets were often made in pairs.

Condition
The condition of goblets is important as many later examples have been subjected to very heavy use and may be damaged beyond repair. In particular, check for:
*splits in the bowl
*splits in the stem
*damage where the bowl joins the stem.

Later Regency goblets were of very high quality and tended to be made by the best makers of time (ie. Paul Storr for Rundell, Bridge and Rundell). This example, made by William Burwash in 1819, is slightly less elaborate than many Regency goblets, but the cast and applied band of grapes and vine leaves around the rim makes it far more expensive than if the decoration were chased. This type of goblet is easily damaged, so check carefully for repairs where the body joins the stem, and make sure the foot has not been pushed up into the base. This example is relatively light – a similar goblet made by Paul Storr would be worth around four times as much.
*Regency goblets were often presented as prizes, so check that an old inscription has not been removed.

JUGS

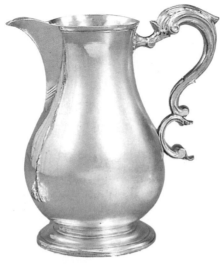

An Irish silver beer jug; Dublin;
1774, ht 8in (20.8cm); 32oz (64dwt); value code C

Identification checklist for a mid-18thC beer jug
1. Is the body baluster-shaped?
2. Does it have a lid?
3. Does it have a central foot?
4. Is there a contemporary coat-of-arms?
5. Is the handle cast?
6. Is the patina suitably aged?
7. Are there no dents to the central belly?
8. Does the jug feel heavy and solid?

Jugs
Large jugs intended for beer or wine came into use with the restoration of Charles II. Some of the early ones have covers, but after the 1730s these are very rare. They do not have insulated handles and were probably never designed to hold anything hot; if a jug has an ivory handle this will have been added later. Most 18thC jugs are baluster-shaped and up until the reign of George II had plain bodies, after which time rococo influences led to more elaborate designs.

Collecting
Unlike tankards which were made in large quantities, beer jugs were far more important pieces of silver, designed to be used in only the grandest homes. Consequently they are far rarer and more expensive today. A good coat-of-arms is a welcome feature on a jug and some of the best examples have cut-card decoration to the lip.

Irish Jugs
Although the Irish jug in the main picture was made in 1774 it is typical of English designs in the mid-18thC, reflecting the usual time delay in English designs reaching Ireland. Fashions also tended to last for longer in Ireland. However, the handle is a little more elaborate than would have been found on English examples – a hint of the Irish fondness for decoration has crept in.

Unusually, this beer jug was made as one of a pair, one engraved "A", the other "B", on the handles. Made in 1733, the jugs are pear-shaped and are decorated with fine early rococo coats-of-arms which are typical of the period. In keeping with tankards of the day (see pp. 88-89), the rest of the body is plain.
*At this time the jugs have covers and are sometimes called hot water jugs. However, the "A" and "B" on these jugs stands for "Ale" and "Beer", a firm indication of their original purpose.
*Any jugs which were made in pairs are particularly desirable.

This later jug from 1835 is decorated with a typical, classical scene of Aurora in her chariot. The applied grape-laden vines around the rim and the base indicate it was used at table to serve wine. These expensive jugs are always heavy and in silver gilt. The fact that this one is by Paul Storr doubles its value.

Shaving Jugs
Shaving jugs are very rare and were made only during the reigns of George I and Queen Anne. This example was made by Simon Pantin in 1717. They always have a cover, but they are smaller than beer jugs and are oval in shape. Again there are no insulation sockets at the handles. Originally they were accompanied by a large oval basin with a cut-out in the border, designed to hold under the chin, but the two parts are frequently separated and the jug sold on its own. Marks and arms on the two items should correspond.

TEA AND COFFEE

A Victorian 4-piece teaset; Joseph & John Angell; London; 1845

Silver items associated with tea and coffee form a major collecting area. Apart from the pots themselves, there is a vast range of objects to choose from – from kettles and urns, sugar and cream jugs, caddies and caddie spoons, to pairs of tongs and teaspoons, teapot stands and spoon trays. All these have survived in England in substantially large numbers, but there are far fewer to be found in the United States (see pp. 148-149).

The earliest 18thC teapots were small because of the high cost of tea, which at this time was still a luxury commodity afforded by only the very rich. Although form changed over the years, decoration remained minimal, largely confined to a little engraving or flat chasing on the shoulder of bullet or Scottish teapots, and some attractive bright-cutting on late 18thC pots. There is a curious gap in the middle of the 18thC when teapots did not seem to have been made in England at all, although they continued to be produced in Scotland.

During this gap in production of teapots in the mid 18thC a number of tea kettles were produced, and later, in the 1760s, these were replaced by tea urns. Tea kettles were obviously expensive due to their size and complexity and the fact that apart from the earliest examples they were profusely decorated with flat-chasing. Most kettles had a salver-like stand which between c.1730-1750 was occasionally triangular in shape. These have rarely survived with the kettle today but occasionally they are offered for sale on their own as trays or waiters.

Although tea urns were made earlier in the 18thC, it was not until the 1760s that they became popular. Some had burners but most had a heated iron bar which fitted into a container inside the body, providing a much cleaner way of heating the water than using a flame. Urns were made in a wide variety of designs but the basic form was always vase- or ovoid-shaped. Although urns and kettles are decorative they are large and take up a lot of space and they are not popular among collectors. As with any silver which has been subjected to a direct source of heat, check carefully for wear; often the marks on the base will have been erased.

Like teapots, coffee pots are largely plain, although a few early examples were engraved with cut-card decoration and some very elaborate rococo pots were produced towards the middle of the 18thC. Both octagonal teapots and coffee pots made at the beginning of the 18thC are particularly sought-after and because they are rare they command high prices. Early coffee pots had raised rather than cast spouts, sometimes with a hinged flap, and sometimes placed at right angles to the handle. Coffee pots were straight-sided until the 1730s when the bellied body with a tuck-in foot appeared, only to be replaced with the vase shape in the 1760s when there was a classical revival. Some elaborate Regency coffee pots have stands and burners. Chocolate pots were only made up until c.1730. They were virtually identical to coffee pots, but they had a hinged or detachable cap or finial in the lid through which a rod was inserted to stir up the chocolate sediment. A knowledge of the shapes of both coffee and tea pots provides a useful aid to dating, but it is important to remember that many 18thC styles were repeated in the 19thC and 20thC, so always check the marks. Although there is nothing wrong with a reproduction, they are worth considerably less than an original.

Tea and coffee services from before the 1790s are rare, and most date from the Victorian times when they were made in an infinite variety, usually very elaborate, and sometimes in fitted wooden chests occasionally complete with matching trays. Because services are available in large numbers and in such a variety of combinations, they are popular among collectors today.

Tea caddies were often expensive and elaborate, again reflecting the high price of tea. Finely engraved coats-of-arms feature prominently on early oblong caddies and the quality of decoration on mid-18thC examples can be very high. From the 1730s caddies are found in pairs with a matching sugar container and some were made to fit into a lockable case. It is interesting to note that caddies themselves acquired locks in the 1760s when tea was no longer such an expensive commodity as it had been earlier on in the century. Although most caddies date from the 18thC a number of small reproductions were made around the beginning of the 20thC but these are less collectable today.

Early 18thC sugar containers are rare. Most date from the end of the century and the combination of a classical shape and attractive engraving makes them very collectable. 18thC cream or milk jugs were produced in a variety of shapes and sizes; early examples had small spouts and were probably used for milk, but from the 1720s onwards jugs with a broader lip, more suitable for cream, were made. One of the more unusual and amusing variations of the cream jug is the cow creamer (see p. 156), made in the 18thC by John Schuppe.

TEAPOTS 1

A rare George I silver teapot; Samuel Wastell, London; 1711; ht 6in (15cm); value code A

Identification checklist for a late 17thC/early 18thC teapot

1. Is it pear-shaped?
2. Does it have a wooden handle and finial? (Here the original handles have been replaced with ivory.)
3. Is the body marked underneath in a line?
4. Is the cover marked with the maker's mark and lion's head erased?
5. Is the hinge on the lid secure?
6. Are the seams free from damage?
7. Is the cover domed?

Early teapots

Early teapots date from the reign of Queen Anne. Tea had only begun to be drunk in quantities at the turn of the 18thC. It was very expensive and this is reflected in the small size of many early teapots (usually between 4½in (15cm) and 6in (150cm) high). Shapes changed quite considerably, from pear-shaped in the early 18thC to bullet-shaped mid-century, and later drum-shaped. Octagonal teapots were only made for a very short time (c.1710-1725) and are very rare and expensive today.

*Early pots had wooden handles and finials; these were replaced with ivory during the Regency period and silver in the 19thC.

Scottish teapots also tend to have silver handles.

Condition

Many teapots have been badly damaged through frequent use. Check the pot for leaks and old repairs at spouts, handles, hinges and for any soldered joins. Most teapots will be stained dark brown inside which may disguise repairs. However, if the inside is shiny the pot may have been restored. The hinge on the lid is a good indicator of wear; if it is tight the rest is probably in good condition. On early examples with wooden handles check the handle is not loose or the wood rotten. Often handles and finials have been replaced.

Flat lids were an early develop-ment but the inverted pear shape of this pot is unusually early. The octagonal spout and handle sock-ets on this example by René Hudell (1719) make it particular-ly desirable. As on later bullet teapots, the band of engraving where the lid comes down on the body cleverly disguises the join.

Bullet teapots

Bullet-shaped teapots were made from c.1730-1745 and are relative-ly rare today. Some were made with a detachable lid, in which case check that it fits properly. Bullet tepots are difficult to sell for a good price unless the lid has a clear maker's mark as well as the lion passant. Some bullet teapots have no side seam; these examples were raised in one piece and the base was put on after the hinge had been fitted to the inside and the lid had been attached. This type nearly always has a loose lid after 250 years of wear and it is virtually impossible to repair the hinge properly.

Decoration

The best-quality bullet-shaped teapots are finely engraved around the shoulder and have a fine coat-of-arms. Less expensive ones will be plain. Early Queen Anne teapots are usually plain, but some fine examples by Huguenot makers are embellished with cut-card work. Much George I domestic silver is unadorned and teapots are no exception, although in the 1730s bullet teapots were often engraved at the shoulders and corner of the lid with bands of masks and strapwork. A good coat-of-arms is a great asset and the removal is noticeable because it is hard to get rid of the dent as it has to be done from inside.

This is a typical bullet teapot of the period with a silver finial on the lid. Sometimes finials can be made of wood with a silver threaded screw and spool-shaped support, and on such examples none of the finials should be missing.

Some British provincial teapots are similar to Scottish ones; this teapot was made in Newcastle in 1757. The unusual spout, encased in a petal wrapping, also featured on examples made in Exeter by Elston and Symonds. Unlike most bullet-shaped teapots, on this example the hinge is easily accessible for repair. Other teapots were made in York from where one or two very attractive late-18thC examples with flat-shaped square sides were made by Hampton and Prince.

TEAPOTS 2

A silver teapot; Hester Bateman;
1780; ht 4½in (11.5cm); value code D

Identification checklist for a late-18thC teapot
1. Is it oval or drum-shaped?
2. Does it have beaded or threaded borders?
3. Is there no evidence of repairs, particularly inside to the base?
4. Is there any wear to the hinge?
5. Does it have a good coat-of-arms? (This one is quite weak which will lower the price.)
6. Is the spout free from splits?
7. Is it not suspiciously shiny inside?

Later teapots
English teapot manufacture resumed in the 1780s. New simple shapes were popular, not only because of the Neo-Classical revival, but also the availability of rolled sheet metal in a light gauge which was very easy to make into oval or circular teapots. Many makers took advantage of these advancements by stepping up production and reducing prices. Although many are attractively decorated, they are not nearly as robust as their predecessors. Not only were the bodies lightly made, the spouts were no longer cast, but instead were made up from sheet metal and seamed together. After constant use the spouts can split along the seam and this is difficult to repair neatly. Also, the end of the spout can be easily damaged. Renewal of arms on this sort of teapot leaves the metal very thin.

Drum-shaped teapots were made for a few years in the 1770s. Some are very small and these are known as bachelor teapots. It is possible to turn this type into a caddy by removing the handle and spout, but the faker will have trouble fitting the lid correctly. These pots are not chased but there is usually a band of attractive engraving at the top and bottom. There are some fakes around so look carefully; the cover should have just a lion passant and the maker's mark.

In the 19thC teapots were often made with separate stands. The outline of the stand should always match that of the teapot and any decoration or coat-of-arms should be identical. Stands were either like the one featured here, made of wood sheathed with silver and without feet, or like the salvers of the time, with feet (see pp. 46-47).
*Bright-cut decoration adds a premium if it is in good condition, but here it is no longer crisp.

Stands
Stands often get separated from their pot and if sold on their own those in the shape of a salver are more popular – when they are usually sold as waiters.

Decoration
Some late-18thC teapots are entirely plain with only a crest or coat-of-arms set between a thread or beaded border. These plain pots tend to be of a heavier gauge than other examples. On other pots engraving or bright-cutting is popular, but frequently this is now in poor condition due to constant use of the pot. On teapots with flush-fitting lids the decoration sometimes overlaps

onto the top of the pot itself. Later teapots have chased decoration; and on those made in the Regency period the decoration was usually cast.

After c.1800 the oval body became oblong and the pot stood on four ball feet. Although this type of teapot is very common and has a more practical capacity than the early small ones, it is probably the least popular among collectors. Examples tend to be of poor quality; the large spout is easily damaged and the hollow ball feet often wear through. The pot tends to be fluted in the corners or have a broad band of alternating lobes and flutes which are likely to develop vertical splits. After this time teapots were usually made in services.

Scottish teapots
Scottish teapots are easily identified by the shape of the body which is either completely spherical like the one below, or slightly flattened. Other distinguishing

features include:
*tall foot
*long spout.
Unlike London teapots, Scottish examples continued to be produced throughout the 18thC.

This teapot made in 1727 is typical of Scottish examples, although many of them have silver handles rather than the wooden one featured here.
*Some later Scottish teapots are decorated with chasing at the shoulders.

COFFEE POTS 1

An 18thC coffee pot; Thomas Farrer; 1730; ht 9½in (24cm); value code C

Identification checklist for an early 18thC coffee pot
1. Are the hallmarks in a line to the right of the handle, or scattered under the foot?
2. Is the lid also marked, with only the lion passant and maker's mark? (Duty mark added after 1784.)
3. Is there a contemporary coat-of-arms on the body?
4. Are the proportions of the pot in keeping with its date? (Odd proportions may indicate the pot is a conversion from a tankard.)
5. If the pot was made in England, does it have a wooden handle? (Silver, ivory or composition handles are usually later replacements and reduce value.)
6. Does the inside of the pot have a dull appearance? (A polished finish could indicate it has been altered in some way.)
7. Is any decoration flat-chased?

Coffee pots
Most coffee and chocolate pots date from c.1700 onwards when these beverages became popular, although examples of earlier ones do exist. They are usually much the same size, but some considerably smaller pots by good makers were produced in the 1700 which are expensive for their size today. Queen Anne pots are of plain form, enlivened only by a coat-of-arms, or occasionally, cut-card decoration.
*Early lids are domed, becoming flat by the 1730s and thereafter rising again until the end of the century.

Armorials
A coat-of-arms or monogram would usually be placed opposite the handle, so that guests would be able to see them when the pot was being used. On the pot in the main picture the arms unusually fill one side. Coffee pots of this date should be carefully examined for evidence of erased or replaced armorials which greatly reduce the value.

The earliest coffee pots, such as this one from 1702, had highly-domed lids; handles were often placed at right angles to the spout and the body was unadorned. The hinged spout flap and decoration on the lid add to the value.
*Coffee pots are extremely popular with collectors and good ones fetch high prices.

Decoration
Decoration became more varied during the 18thC. Flat-chased bands around the top and bottom of a pot were typical embellishments in the 1740s, as were asymmetric cartouches and tuck-in feet. Irish coffee pots were often covered in chased decoration. In England however, all-over shell and flower scroll decoration did not become prevalent until the Victorian period.

By the 1740s coffee pots had tuck-in feet. This example has typical decoration of the time with a band of flat chasing around the bottom and the top of the body and round the cartouche. The elaborate spout is leaf-wrapped to balance the scrolling socket handle. Check the cartouche to see that a coat-of-arms has not been removed.
*Most English coffee pots had elegant wooden handles; it it likely that the handle on this pot has been replaced a factor which will lower its value.

Chocolate pots
Chocolate pots were made in identical styles and designs to coffee pots, but with hinged finials. These could be lifted and a rod or stick inserted to stir the chocolate to prevent it from separating. This chocolate pot dating from 1715 has a hinged finial attached by a captive chain to prevent its loss. The quality of the pot is further reflected in the reinforced handle sockets, which help bear the weight when the full pot is lifted.

Marks
On chocolate pots, marks on the detachable finials are desirable although not essential.

COFFEE POTS 2

A late 18thC coffee pot, James Young;
1769; ht 9½in (24cm); value code C

Identification checklist for a late-18thC coffee pot
1. Is the body baluster-shaped or pear-shaped?
2. Does the pot stand on a spreading foot?
3. Does it have a stepped and domed lid?
4. Is there any gadrooning on the rims on the foot and on the body?
5. Is the spout in the shape of a bird's beak?

Later coffee pots
By the middle of the 18thC coffee pots had become baluster-shaped and had higher-domed lids than earlier examples. Surprisingly, chased coffee pots are usually less sought-after than plain ones unless the decoration is of exceptional quality. Although the coffee pot in the main picture is slightly dented it is worth significantly more than the one on the right. The damage makes little difference to the value; it could be easily removed.

Value
Value is dependent on a combination of elegance and quality. A good maker, weight and colour make a significant difference to the price.

This coffee pot, made in 1765, has a raised foot and is elaborately decorated with a chased floral design. It is unusual to find the decoration covering the entire body on a piece made before the Victorian period, but the pattern on this example is contemporary with the pot – Victorian chasing would have a more mechanical appearance.

Restoration

It is important to make sure that when coffee pots are restored they are not over-polished in the process; this can wear away the metal and detract from the decoration and surface patina. Always try to repair an old handle. A new one takes very many years to tone down and blend in.

Collecting

Before buying a pot of the type on the left there are several points to look for:
*check plain surfaces for removed arms
*make sure the arms are in keeping with the period (pp. 14-15)
*check whether the hinge needs repairing
*examine handle sockets for evidence of wear; they may need re-pinning.

Gadroon borders are a distinctive feature of many coffee pots made in the 1760s. Pots such as this one which are usually solidly-made and of good quality, are very popular with collectors. The bird's head spout is both decorative and practical; it was made using the casting technique and would be difficult to damage.

Towards the end of the 18thC vase-shaped coffee pots became fashionable. This design has dual appeal because it may be used as either a jug (for hot water) or as a coffee pot. Other features typical of the period are:
*beaded, thread or reeded borders – here the lid is decorated with a beaded border while the foot is edged with a reeded one.
*bright-cut engraving – indicative of finer-quality pots
*ivory handles – these tend to crack but this does not usually affect the value unless they are particularly unsightly.

Hot water jugs

This pot made in 1751 would be more correctly described as a "jug" since it has a lip rather than a spout. Pots of this form were termed hot water jugs and are considerably less valuable than pots with spouts. Even though the gadroon border and acorn finial are signs of good quality, this jug may be worth less than half as much as the pot illustrated in the main picture.
*It is possible that these jugs were made in and used for Turkish coffee which would be better poured from a lip.

TEA SERVICES

*A typical George IV tea service;
c.1823; value code C*

Identification checklist for a George IV tea service
1. Is the set heavy?
2. Are all the pieces identically marked?
3. Are all the detachable pieces – lids, bases, burner – all part-marked to match?
4. Does the design correspond to the period?
5. Is the fluting free from damage? (Splits or lead solder repairs.)
6. Is the body thin where a coat-of-arms has been removed?
7. Are the hinges tight?

Tea services
Although matching tea items were made at the beginning of the 18thC the idea of a tea service did not become popular until c.1790. However, there is an abundant supply and a correspondingly high demand. Most are bought for display purposes. Designs tend to follow the fashions of silver of the time, so tea services were elegant and bright-cut in the 1790s, solid and richly-decorated in the Regency period and mass-produced with lavish decoration during the reign of Queen Victoria.
*The tea service above has a raised central foot which is more hard-wearing than those which stand on four feet.

Collecting
A three-piece tea service consists of a teapot, sugar bowl and cream jug and a four-piece set includes a coffee pot. However, there are many variations and generally the more pieces there are the more desirable the set is – other items include tea kettles, hot milk jugs and water jugs. A set is always worth more than the value of its individual items. Many sets in the past were presented as prizes; any with a lengthy inscription are undesirable.

Condition
A teapot is the most-used part of a set and its state of wear is a good guide to the condition of the set. Check for damage to the feet which are particularly fragile, and for repairs to the body with lead solder which may be hidden in the chasing. Victorian eagle finials often get damaged and as the pattern was also made in plate a silver pot may have a plated finial – any detachable finial should be hallmarked.

This rare early tea service by Peter and Anne Bateman (1791) is decorated with bright-cut engraving which is typical of the period. Several features add to its desirability:
*elegant shape
*matching coats-of-arms on all pieces
*bright-cutting in good condition
The set has a matching caddy which is unusual.

The design of this tea service was very popular during the mid-19thC. This example, made by Roberts & Hall of Sheffield, is a

three-piece set with an additional hot water jug. The jug and coffee pot illustrated here show the difference between a jug, which has a lip, and a pot which has a spout – pots are always more desirable and as here usually have a highly decorative spout.

Victorian and later tea services
Most tea services which come on the market today are from the Victorian period or later. The elaborate repoussé and chased decoration of bucolic scenes on the six-piece set featured below, from 1877, is after the artist Teniers, and was first adopted as a design on tea services by Edward Farrell, a well-known maker in the 1820s. The set is typically heavy and of high quality.
*Make sure every item is marked with the same date and maker as this pattern was produced by more than one workshop.
*As with any high-relief decoration, check the high points, such as the figures, for any wear on details.
*Later tea services sometimes come complete with matching large trays.

TEA CADDIES 1

A George III tea caddy in a silver-mounted tortoiseshell case, Daniel Smith & Robert Sharp; London; 1766; box 10¼in (26cm) long; value code C

Identification checklist for a George III tea caddy
1. Is there a full set of hallmarks on the base of each of the caddies?
2. Is the cover of each caddy marked with the maker's mark and lion passant?
3. Are the coat-of-arms contemporary to the piece?
4. Is there any damage to the feet?
5. Are the finials intact?
6. Is the tortoiseshell veneer complete on the case?
7. Do the caddies fit into the case properly?
8. Does any crest or coat-of-arms on the case match that on the caddies?

Early caddies
The earliest caddies date from the reign of Queen Anne when tea had become a more popular drink. Because tea was a luxury item caddies tended to be well-made and are expensive today. Early caddies are oblong or oval with a sliding base and a detachable lid which was used as a measure for the tea. By about 1780 the cap measure was replaced by the caddy spoon (see p. 171). Early caddies would have had a lead lining but they are very rarely found intact today. Many caddies are quite plain and offer a good surface for arms or a crest.

Later caddies
Initially caddies came in pairs for the two types of tea available at that time – Black and Green – but by the middle of the 18thC they were made with a bowl, initially thought to be for mixing the tea but now generally believed to be for holding sugar. Caddies also came in cased sets and the boxes that held the caddies are often works of art in themselves (see above). At the end of the 18thC caddies had locks, although this is surprising as by this time tea was no longer as expensive as earlier in the century. By the late 18thC caddies were much larger and

were made singly; sometimes they had an internal dividing sheet so that they could hold two different types of tea. Pairs are more desirable than singles, but single caddies are more acceptable than most other silver items that were originally made in pairs.

Condition
Later caddies were sometimes less robust and should be checked carefully for splits in the sides and for cracks in the feet.

The caddy below dates from 1729 and is a much more practical shape than the previous type. Instead of having a sliding lid and a detachable cap this example has a hinged lid. This not only means it cannot get lost, but also that the tea can be put in and taken out from the top.

This caddy from 1714 is a most desirable shape and this is reflected in the price. Each caddy should have a full set of hallmarks on the body and the maker's mark and lion's head on the base. Although the cover on this caddy is marked, this is not always the case with early caddies.

This is the first type of tea caddy likely to be found in a cased set, as a pair, normally together with a larger sugar container. In keeping with the plain shape of the caddy, the case would also have been very simple with a plain veneer and a lock to prevent pilfering. Later examples were far more elaborate. Although the cap on the previous style of caddy was used for measuring tea, the caddy spoon does not feature until the 1770s. A set made Paul de Lamerie in 1701 includes a pair of cups and 13 identical tea spoons, which implies that teaspoons must have been used as measures.

Rococo-style caddies
This fine set of three mid-18thC caddies shows the silversmith taking full advantage of the rococo revival and Chinoiserie decoration popular at the time. Close examination of the detail will enable you to see if it has been cast or chased. If cast, the panels will be identical to each other, and if simply chased there will be minor differences. In addition cast caddies will feel much heavier.

This pair of George III octagonal caddies was made in 1775 by James Phipps. They are complete with a contemporary gilt painted lacquer case with a hinged scroll handle and fitted interior. This type of case is very rare and not long after this date caddies acquired locks and the case became redundant altogether. Also by this time, sugar was being served from baskets and the need for a separate bowl with the caddies had disappeared.

Chasing

Chased decoration tends to be less popular on silver than a good plain surface and will only add to the value if it is in very good condition. It features on a number of tea caddies. Check carefully for solder repairs and any holes to high relief decoration.

thinly-stamped and these are susceptible to damage.
*The highly decorative finial is also prone to damage and should be checked for solder repairs.

The rectangular form of this caddy from 1764 remained popular into the 1770s. The caddy would have originally been part of a set of three with another caddy and a sugar box. The restrained chasing is typical of the period. Check all the way up the corners for signs of repair.

Damage

This type of caddy was made at the time that rolled silver was popular. Some examples may be t

Samuel Taylor made this tea caddy in 1756 and the shape and chased decoration is typical of both the maker (who is very well-known for this type of work), and the period. The foot is cast and very difficult to damage; but the applied leaves on the cover are often incomplete. Although the decoration is fairly elaborate there is still room for a coat-of-arms. Despite the amount of work that has gone into these caddies they are not very popular due to the overall chasing. They were made in sets of three, with a larger, shallower covered bowl.

The caddy illustrated below is very typical of those made in the late 18thC in large numbers and with few variations. Occasionally they were made as part of a teaset. All of these caddies are decorated with bright-cut engraving. On some examples the oval body is ribbed in panels. These caddies were made up from sheet

This type of caddy is invariably of good quality and is very popular with collectors. This example was made by Vere and Lutwyche in 1770. The decoration is Oriental in inspiration. The teaplant-shaped cast finial is attached by a screw and sometimes pieces of the plant have broken off. The engraving is a very prominent feature on these caddies. The design of Chinese cyphers was taken from the chests in whichtea was imported into Britain. The design is sometimes found upside down, reflecting which way up the engraver held his instructions to copy the pattern. Unlike the hinge on caddy on the right which is often loose, the concealed hinge on these examples does not usually need attention.

*This type of caddy is generally sold individually.

metal, and tend to be lightweight so they can be badly worn. The hinge is at the back of the lid and can be over-stressed; it is very hard to repair a loose lid well so any in this condition should be avoided. These caddies had a lock, but they rarely have a key, and the lock itself may be missing. Finials are usually detachable; they are quite plain compared to earlier examples and can be made of wood, silver, or in green stained ivory – in this case in the shape of a pineapple

Scottish tea caddies

Scottish caddies from before the reign of George IV are very rare. This one from 1818 is profusely chased like much silver of the

time. Some may have a division, which should be part-marked. Check for wear at the hinge and on the chasing, and make sure the feet have not collapsed.

These Scottish caddies are large and some have had spout and handles added to make them into teapots which at this time were about the same size as caddies. However, there will be the usual dificulties with hallmarking. This caddy has a swing handle, never seen on 18thC examples, and a lock, which by this time was no longer a necessary feature.

SUGAR BOWLS AND BASKETS

A George III silver sugar basket; William Abdy, London; 1798; lgth 6½ in (16.5cm); value code E.

Identification checklist for a late 18thC sugar basket
1. Is the basket fully marked?
2. Is the handle also marked?
3. Is any coat-of-arms or crest on the body original?
4. Does it have a central foot?
5. Are the handle joints free from damage?
6. Are the handles unbroken?
7. Does the basket measure approximately 6½in (16.5cm) in length?

Development of styles
Sugar was originally kept in silver sugar boxes which first appeared at the end of the 17thC and continued into the reign of Queen Anne. As much of the sugar was cultivated in the West Indies it is not surprising that a number of these boxes appear in the United States. By the beginning of the 18thC sugar was kept in silver bowls, many of which had a reversible cover, probably for holding a spoon. By the middle of the 18thC the covers developed cone finials and thereafter the bodies became vase-shaped with covers that were sometimes cut to

hold spoons. In the 1770s the vases lost their covers and the bowls were eventually replaced by larger, open sugar baskets, before being made as part of tea sets (see pp. 106-107).

The basket in the main picture is most frequently sold either as a sugar or sweetmeat basket. Sometimes these late tea baskets are fitted with a glass liner, even though the bodies seldom have any piercing until the Victorian times. The body of this good-quality example is undecorated but most of them are engraved with bright-cutting.
*Avoid any light-weight baskets.

Sugar vase
This sugar vase represents the final development of the sugar bowl with a cover (slightly earlier ones were identical to the tea caddies of the time, see p. 110).

This early sugar bowl, made by James Goodwin in 1726, is typically plain, although some examples do have a crest or coat-of-arms. Check that the marks on the cover match those on the bowl and avoid buying simply the base on its own. These bowls are very rare.

The basket below is an attractive Victorian example not made as part of a teaset. It was made in 1857 by Barnard Bros. The coloured glass liner is difficult to replace. Check carefully for broken parts in the piercing.

This example by Paul de Lamerie (1746) would have been made as part of a set with two caddies. These vases are generally good quality and of the same shape. This example is decorated with shells, but leaves, rams' masks and drapery are also popular. Some may have the cover cut to accommodate a sugar ladle although the spoon is frequently missing – de Lamerie has made the spoon as well as the vase, but this is unusual. The marks are very worn on this example which reduces the value considerably.

Irish sugar bowls
Quite large numbers of Irish sugar bowls appear on the market, made in either Dublin or, as in the case of this example from c.1760, in Cork. Irish provincial silver always commands a premium and it is much sought-after by collectors. All Irish sugar bowls tend to look similar. They usually have chased decoration of flowers and scrolls.

The feet are headed by human or animal masks. The gauge of the metal is often quite lightweight and many are in relatively poor condition, so check carefully for any holes and damage to the feet, and for repairs to the turned-over rim.

TEA URNS

*An 18thC-style tea urn; 1875;
18in (44.5cm) high; value code D*

Identification checklist for an 18thC or 19thC tea urn
1. Is it fully marked either on the underneath (if
Georgian) or on the body (if Victorian)?
2. Is the cover part-marked with the maker's mark, lion
passant and sovereign's head?
3. Is there no evidence of the internal fittings having
been removed?
4. Is there no sign of any visible repairs? (Taps and
spouts are especially vulnerable.)
5. If the base is separate has it been marked?
6. Does the tap work? (Although this is desirable it is
not essential.)

Tea urns
Tea urns were made from the
1760s onwards, and were probably used for holding hot water to
replenish the pot rather than for
tea itself. Although a few urns
have burners most, especially
plated examples, have a
cylindrical inner sleeve to hold a
hot iron bar, which proved to be
just as effective as a burner. Sizes
and shapes vary greatly and there
is no such thing as a "typical" tea
urn. Despite their variety and
decorative qualities, urns are not
especially popular with collectors
and they remain relatively
inexpensive today.

This unusually early tea urn from the late 1760s is decorated with typical mid-18thC chased scrolls and blooms, but the Chinoiserie

figures add greatly to its value. The urn is supported on an elaborately pierced separate base. Initially urns had charcoal burners, internal hollow flues that heated the water, and no internal fittings. Always check any open-work for any cracks and damage caused by the heat.

Regency tea urns of this type are particularly expensive. This one made by Paul Storr for Rundell Bridge & Rundell in c.1810 has a stand integral to the body. The band of anthemion decoration is

typical. Quality features include elaborately-cast feet and handles, the ivory palmette-shaped handle and the marks of a good maker.

Tea kettles

Tea kettles made for boiling water at the table date from the 1730s. They comprise two or three parts – kettle, stand and a burner which is sometimes separate. These are much smaller than tea urns and usually have a lower capacity and weigh considerably less. Early examples are circular and relatively plain in form. The one featured below, made in 1742 by Thomas Farren, is the most popular type made in the mid-18thC. It has a swing handle and fairly plain body adorned only with a coat-of-arms and relatively restrained chased

decoration. The decorative apron surrounding the stand is cast and parts of it can easily break off. *Kettles are marked underneath and the marks have often been made illegible by the flame from the burner.

Reproductions

Tea kettles waned in popularity after c.1760 although they reappeared in the mid-Victorian period as part of tea sets. The 19thC urn in the main picture is a late-Victorian copy of a 1780s example. It reflects the classical styles popular in the late 18thC and is decorated with a beaded border typical of the century, but the proportions and the slightly clinical look identify it as a Victorian copy.

CREAM JUGS 1

A cream jug; Francis Crump, London; 1742; ht 4½in (11.5cm)

Identification checklist for an 18thC cream jug
1. Is it fully marked in a group underneath?
2. Does the body stand on a rim foot?
3. Is the form simple?
4. Is there any decoration on the body?
5. Does it feel solid to hold?
6. Are there any join lines visible on the inside? (If so, the jug has been cast.)

Milk jugs

Milk jugs were first made in the early years of the 18thC. Those made during the reign of Queen Anne follow the lines of tea pots of the period (see pp. 98-101). Some early jugs were made with lids and had wooden handles. These were used for serving warm milk rather than cream. From c.1720 onwards milk or cream was served cold and jugs became smaller, the lids disappeared and silver replaced wood as the material for handles.
*By the end of the 18thC milk and cream jugs were usually made as part of tea sets, generally by the same makers who produced teapots. The jug illustrated in the main picture is a good-quality early 18thC example.
*Some early 18thC cream jugs have cast bodies and on these the join lines are sometimes visible down the inside of the body.

Marks

Milk jugs are marked either on their side or underneath. Early marks have frequently been faked or inserted by duty dodgers. A reassuring sign of authenticity is to see the marks underneath the body from inside as this indicates that a disc of fake marks has not not been inserted.

Beware
Conversions of less desirable or useful pieces of silver into practical and collectable milk jugs abound. Not all are intended to deceive but among the wares most commonly converted into milk jugs are:
*pepper casters
*christening mugs.

Hot milk jugs, such as this one which was made in 1709, are extremely rare and are among the most valuable of milk jugs. They are significantly larger than the cream jugs which followed them and considerably heavier; this one is 6⅛in (15.6cm) high and weighs 13 oz (4dwt) and is worth many times more than the jug in the main picture opposite.
*Hot milk jugs should be fully marked underneath the base, and also part marked on the cover. They should also have the lion's head erased for the Britannia period (1697-1719).

Octagonal cream jugs, such as this one made by William Looker of London in 1716, are also highly desirable and are worth

substantially more than plain baluster-shaped examples of the same date.
*The high quality of this jug is reflected in the well-moulded spout and the wire-reinforced rim which also add to its durability.

This typical pitcher cream jug of 1730 made by Elizabeth Goodwin is of fine quality but, as with any jug, should be checked for the following signs of weakness:
*foot pushed into the body
*splits in rim
*signs of an erased crest.
*repairs to the handle sockets.
Because this jug is one of the most desirable of the early styles it has occasionally been faked in the past, sometimes from the bottom of a caster of the period with adjustments for the base and a new handle and lip.

The jug illustrated below, from c.1745, is one of a number of similar high-quality cast cream boats and jugs which are particularly sought-after today. Most of them are unmarked, but there is a small group of makers to which they can be ascribed. Among its desirable features are:
*a cast body, foot and handle
*a lavish cast and applied decoration on the side of the body
*an unusually elaborate handle
*a gilded finish.

CREAM JUGS 2

A mid-18thC milk jug;
1751, 4in (10cm) high; value code F

Identification checklist for a mid-18thC milk jug
1. Is the jug fully marked underneath?
2. If it is lidded, does the lid also bear some marks?
3. Is the handle cast?
4. Are the rim, handle and base free of damage?
5. Is the crest the original?
6. Are the feet not pushed up into the body?

Later milk jugs

After the introduction of a separate foot to cream jugs in the 1730s the form became more varied – the cream boat on p. 117 and the cow creamer on p. 176 show two extremes of design. The helmet-shaped jug, always well-suited for pouring cream, was produced in quantity in Ireland. Many Irish jugs are heavily chased with 18thC flowers, and the feet are typically headed by lion's masks. Although they are usually of a good gauge, these jugs often have splits at the plain waved rim. Sometimes they have been repaired, but the solder shows up if breathed upon. English helmet jugs at the end of the century may be fluted, but most are simply engraved. After this time jugs were made in sets.

Some very elaborately-decorated milk jugs were produced from the mid-18thC onwards with cast handles and feet. This one, made in 1747 by Benjamin Godfrey, has a chased baluster body and an equally lavishly worked vine pattern handle which has been typically cast.

*The chasing should be checked for repairs. Holes are often blocked with lead solder applied from the inside. Lead solder is grey and easily visible if the silver is cleaned.

*This basic shape with a taller foot and simpler handle continued to be produced until the end of the 18thC.

This distinctive helmet-shaped cream jug on three feet is a characteristically Irish style. As with much Irish silver of the mid-18thC the jug is without a date letter, although stylistically it can be dated to c.1760. Most pieces are of good quality and considerably larger and heavier than their English counterparts. This one has plain feet, but on many Irish wares the feet are surmounted by lion's masks. As with any silver,

the mark of a well known maker can add considerably to the value. This elegant vase-shaped cream jug is marked by Hester Bateman, the best known female silversmith of the 18thC, and is worth twice as much as a jug by any ordinary maker.

*This type of jug can also be found with bright-cut engraved decoration which adds significantly to the value.

*The beading is typical of the 1780s. These jugs could also have a thread or reeded border in the 1790s, and some were also decorated with batswing fluting, so-called because of the waved tops to the flutes.

Cream pails

Elegant pierced cream pails with glass liners became fashionable during the 1770s and are very rare and highly sought-after by today's collectors.

This particularly fine example of an early cream pail has attractive piercing that includes dogs and cats in the decoration. As with any type of openwork the piercing should be carefully examined for repairs and cracks. Handles and feet are particularly prone to damage – later versions had practical swing handles.

Marks

Cream pails are likely to be marked on the flange underneath in a line.

Collecting

Cream jugs are widely available in a variety of styles and shapes, and because (apart from early rare examples made for milk) they are reasonably affordable, they provide an ideal and interesting collecting area. They may be effectively displayed in a cabinet, and most can still be used for practical purposes.

*Any damaged or altered pieces should be avoided because there is still a steady supply of jugs in excellent condition to choose from.

TEAPOTS

Early teapots had a very small capacity, as until the reign of George III tea was an extremely expensive commodity. The early Queen Anne pear shape soon gave way to the bullet-shaped teapot which was made from c.1730-1745. By the end of the 18thC teapots had become drum-shaped or oval and were now of a larger capacity. At the beginning of the 19thC the pots were even larger and now stood on four ball feet. After this time teapots continued to be made, but generally as part of services.

c.1725

c..1725

c.1730

1735 (Scottish)

c.1750

c.1770

c.1795

c.1810

c.1810

COFFEE POTS

Early coffee pots from the beginning of the 18thC had a cylindrical body and a handle at an angle to the body and a high dome cover. (Lids became gradually flatter as the century progressed.) These early pots were also referred to as chocolate pots. From c.1730 coffee pots became baluster-shaped until 1800, after which time they were vase-shaped. Like teapots coffee pots then became oblong before being made in teasets in the Victorian

c.1708

c.1720

c.1725

c.1730

c.1740

c.1755

times when they then followed the style of the set.

One of the simplest ways of dating a coffee pot is by the shape of the body and the height of the lid. Vase-shaped pots are popular, and as with most other items of silver any octagonal pots are particularly sought-after and will command a premium. Irish pots tend to follow the same styles, but slightly later.

c.1765

c.1770

1775

c.1795

c.1810

c.1815

WINE

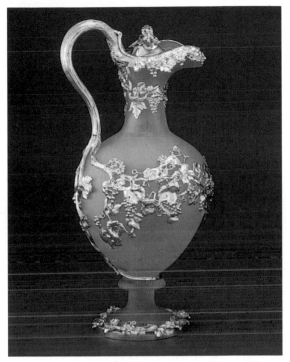

A Victorian silver-mounted claret jug; Mortimer & Hunt; c.1840

Since the 1760s wine has been an increasingly popular drink in Britain and consequently most silver items associated with the wine trade have been produced in large quantities and are quite readily available today. Associated items include wine coasters for holding the glass decanters, silver labels for wine bottles, and wine funnels for decanting the wine.

18thC wine bottles did not have paper labels and the need to know the contents of the bottle after it had been removed from the bin led to the introduction of the silver wine label in the 1740s. This is one of the few collecting areas where the earliest examples are by no means the most expensive. Prices depend far more on the subject and the decoration. Popular titles such as Port, Brandy, Sherry and Claret are more readily saleable because unlike obscure names they can be used on present-day decanters. Gin is sometimes spelt backwards as "Nig", perhaps to confuse the servants or to gloss over the drinking of such a common tipple! Labels are generally hung from a chain; others are suspended from a wire hoop which slips over the neck of the bottle, but the presence of chain or hoop makes little difference to value as modern replacements can be easily made. Smaller silver labels were also produced in large numbers for sauce bottles.

Wine was decanted through a silver funnel. These are nearly always plain, with only a decorative border for variety. Although the rare early 18thC examples have straight spouts later ones have the spout turned to the side to allow the wine to trickle down the side of the decanter. Many spouts have been trimmed straight and these should be avoided.

English wine tasters of the type with a domed centre are very rare. However small two-handled dishes were made in large numbers in the second half of the 17thC which were frequently described as tasters but which could have equally well been sweetmeat dishes. One such small dish is the earliest known piece of American silver.

Wine coasters were made in huge numbers from the reign of George II onwards. Most of them have wooden bases, sometimes with a crested silver disc; more expensive variations have silver bottoms which should be separately marked. Some very expensive and heavy silver gilt coasters were made in the Regency times with the sides cast in sections.

A number of novelty silver wine vessels are of interest to the collector. The need for passing two bottles round a table at the same time (presumably Port and Madeira) led to the 18thC introduction of the jolly boat, an open double stand on four small caster, and the decanter trolley, basically a pair of coasters joined by a wheeled chassis with a handle at the front. When buying such items check that all the individual pieces are marked.

Silver wine jugs for serving wine came into fashion in c.1830, usually decorated with appropriate vine motifs. (Coasters for holding decanters continued to be produced throughout the 19thC which suggests the two vessels were used together.) Solid-bodied examples were followed a little later by glass jugs with silver mounts. These are popular as they can look very decorative on a table. Plain glass bodies are not as popular as frosted or engraved examples, and in general the more elaborate the glass the higher the quality of the mounts. Particularly sought-after jugs include some made in the 1880s with "rock crystal" bodies and the Cellini (see p. 127) and the Armada jugs, both of which are very decorative.

Wine coolers mostly date from the second half of the 18thC, but a number were produced before the 1770s. They were made in pairs and are surprisingly plentiful for such expensive objects. Most are based on the vase or bucket shape, but some were made in imitation of the Warwick vase. Classical motifs feature strongly on the massive Regency coolers of Rundell, Bridge and Rundell, whereas Victorian coolers revert to more naturalistic decoration. A number of Sheffield plate wine coolers are sold without their lids and collars, and although these are worth considerably less than a complete silver example, they make attractive flower vases.

CLARET JUGS

A silver-mounted claret jug;
1870; ht 11in (28cm); value code D/E

Identification checklist for a 19thC claret jug
1. Is the body fully marked and the cover part-marked?
2. If the foot is silver-mounted does it too bear marks?
3. Is the glass original, and almost certainly decorated in some way? (Plain glass bodies can be suspect.)
4. Does the glass fit the mount perfectly? (An ill-fitting body may be a replacement.)
5. Is the hinge on the lid undamaged?
6. If the handle is made from silver is it in good condition?
7. If the handle is made from glass is it free from chips and cracks?

Claret jugs
Silver mounted glass claret jugs became fashionable in the middle of the 19thC, when they were produced in substantial numbers. The silver mounts were often highly elaborately decorated, but the quality may vary – they are frequently stamped from thin metal and may become easily worn. Plated claret jugs were also popular; most of them were of utilitarian quality, although the firm of Elkington & Co. produced some fine examples with parcel gilt mounts. Claret jugs do not follow any set pattern of shapes and they were made in

a wide variety of novel forms such as birds, fish and monkeys. Silver mounted decanters were also made but with the exception of grand Regency examples, they tend to be less sought-after.

Glass bodies
The glass body of claret jugs was usually etched or engraved with some form of decoration and is often elaborately shaped. The body in the main picture is embellished with gilded stars and the base is cut with a star pattern. A plain glass body is likely to be a replacement. The condition of the glass is of fundamental importance to the value, since replacing a broken glass may be impossible.

Decoration on the mounts which corresponds to that on the body is a reassuring indication that everything belongs together. On this claret jug from 1887 the diamond and flower pattern on the mount is mirrored in the decoration on the glass body and on the foot. Silver bases such as the one on this example, may have been added later to hide a chipped glass base, so check the body carefully and make sure the jug does not leak.
*Jugs which have coloured glass bodies are likely to be Continental.

The renaissance-inspired Cellini pattern ewer (pictured above) and the Armada pattern jug were two standard all-silver designs of claret jug which were made throughout the second half of the 19thC. All follow the same shape and can have self-opening lids. They tend to be marked in a line close to the neck and on Cellini jugs the marks are often hidden in the decoration. Many Cellini jugs were made in Glasgow. They are often gilded and tend to be relatively small but some are cast and heavy. The stamped decoration on Armada jugs is frequently of inferior quality.
*Large cartouches on either side of the jugs were invariably engraved with inscriptions or armorials and blank ones should be carefully examined for signs of any erasures.
*Solid-bodied claret jugs are not as popular as glass-bodied ones as the colour of the wine cannot be seen through the metal.

Condition
The damage to solid-bodied claret jugs is similar to that which occurs on glass-bodied examples (see above). Poor design can lead to damage to the handle as some of these jugs are very heavy when full. Likewise, feet can be pushed up into the body and this is difficult to repair, particularly on jugs with a narrow neck.

WINE COASTERS

A pair of wine coasters; Paul Storr;
1810; value code C

Identification checklist for an 18thC wine coaster

1. Is the wine coaster fully hallmarked on the rim on the base?
2. Is the border not damaged or excessively worn? Has the wood remained in reasonable condition?
3. Is there no damage to the silver where it turns over the wooden base?

If there is a central boss:

4. Is it marked? (Preferable but not essential.)
5. Does it have a crest or coat of arms? (Only if it has a silver base.)

Wine coasters

Wine coasters were first made in c.1760 when they had wooden bases and intricately pierced bodies, often incorporating a small medallion for a crest. Later in the 18thC the sides of coasters were made of sheet metal pierced with geometric motifs or festoons, or sometimes bright-cut engraving. The wooden bases were now centered with a silver boss to hold the crest. The boss should bear the lion passant mark, and possibly a maker's mark. Check that the crest is contemporary as any which have been added at a later date are undesirable. Among the most sumptuous coasters are those made in the Regency period with silver bases.

*Coasters were designed to hold decanters rather than bottles.
*Early wine coasters tend to have slightly higher sides than later examples

This coaster from 1770 is typical of the earliest examples, and has a plain, flat wooden base rather than the turned wooden base of the later example in the main picture above. The relatively high sides, wavy border and elaborate openwork are also typical characteristics of earlier coasters.

*Openwork of the type seen on this coaster is fragile and needs careful examination to ensure there are no cracks, missing pieces or signs of repair.

Condition

The condition of the wood does not greatly affect value but can indicate how much wear a coaster has received. In the example in the main picture the wood is quite shiny showing it has not been over-used. In worn pieces the patina of the wood tends to be removed by absorbing wine .
*The underneath of the bases are covered in green baize to prevent the coasters from scratching the surface of furniture.

Simpler coasters, adorned only with a band of bright-cut decoration, were popular towards the end of the 18thC. This pair of coasters from 1796 has much lower sides than the one illustrated bottom left. Coasters of this form were made in large numbers with both plain and pierced sides until the style in the main picture took over.

Marks

Most coasters are marked on the plain lower rim which overlaps the wooden base and those that have been well-used often have badly worn marks that are difficult to read. Very early coasters are marked in the piercing and the marks may be hard to find.

Collecting

Coasters are widely available but, because they can still be used, are still expensive. They were always made in pairs or larger sets; single ones are undesirable and worth a quarter of the value of a pair. A well-known maker can also add to the value – the pair in the main picture are by Paul Storr and are therefore highly collectable.

The most opulent Regency coasters were made from silver gilt, with heavy cast sides and a sheet of silver on the bases, which were engraved with coats-of-arms. The exceptional quality of this pair of coasters is characteristic of the royal goldsmiths Rundell, Bridge & Rundell for whom most coasters of this type were made. These are among the most valuable available and would be worth many times more than the one illustrated in the main picture on the opposite page.

Coasters with stamped sides were inexpensively produced in large quantities in the Victorian period. These Gothic-style coasters, made by Henry Wilkinson & Co. of Sheffield in 1843, probably have hollow borders and will not withstand excessive wear. In the later 19thC coasters with high, pierced sides became popular once again.

WINE FUNNELS

A wine funnel; Eames and Barnard, London; 1819; 5¼ in (13cm) high; value code F

Identification checklist for an 18thC wine funnel
1. Are the bowl and spout marked by the same maker and in the same year.
2. Has the spout been trimmed?
3. Is there of sign of any repairs where the hook joins the body?
4. Is the body plain?
5. Is any crest original?
6. Is there any damage to the piercing in the strainer?

Wine funnels
Wine funnels were used to decant wine from the bottle for serving it at the table. Although they were made as early as 1700 they do not appear in quantity until c.1770. Late 18thC examples were made in two parts – a bowl and funnel. The bowl is pierced to strain any sediment from the wine. Where the two pieces join there is sometimes a plain circular ring which slots in between. This would have had muslin tied to it for extra efficiency but it has not often survived. Many wine funnels originally had stands but very few are found complete with these today. Considering the elaborate decoration on almost everything else connected with the drink trade, it is a surprising that funnels are so plain.

Marks
The bowl, spout and circular disc of wine funnels should all be marked. However, because the funnels were used so often the marks are often badly worn or even missing.

Alterations

The wine funnel in the main picture is typical of those made from the end of the 18thC onwards which had spouts that curved off to one side so that the wine would trickle own the side of the decanter. The necks of decanters gradually became narrower and in order to fit the funnel into the vessel the curved spouts were trimmed down. An untrimmed funnel is far more desirable than a trimmed one.

This funnel was made in Dublin in 1808. It is of a similar style to the one in the main picture but has had its spout trimmed down so that it will fit into the narrow neck of the decanter. Although this will reduce the price, it does make the funnel easier to use but even if it is in excellent condition purist collectors will shun it.

This Dublin wine funnel from 1838 has managed to retain its stand. The stand is slightly raised in the centre and was designed to catch the drips from the funnel. The construction of this funnel is different from the two previous examples which are made in two parts – in this case the body is made in one piece and it will have a pierced inner liner which lifts out. The shell hook was a popular decorative device at this time. The ribs down the side of the spout not only serve to strengthen the piece, but help to hold it away from the sides of the decanter and also let the air out when the funnel is used.
*A good funnel and stand is always a popular piece, but something of a rarity. Stands on their own are attractive, but not much use because of the raised centre.

Wine tasters

Two types of wine taster were made in the 17thC. Those with a plain circular body with a dome in the centre so that the colour of the wine could be seen are very rare. Far more common are wine tasters like the one illustrated here, which was made in London in 1661. These do not have a domed centre, so it would not be possible to examine the colour of the wine. They are usually far more decorative than the other style – the chasing on this example is typical.

*Like much Restoration silver this taster is rather lightweight, as there was a shortage of silver.
*Check for splits in the body and tears at the handle sockets.
*French wine tasters were also made. These are plainer and have a deeper bowl and only one handle.

131

WINE LABELS

A silver wine label, Charles Rawlings; London; 1821; value code H

Identification checklist for a wine label
1. Is the decoration crisp?
2. Do details of the decoration show through to the back? (If so it has been stamped.)
3. Is it cast? (And therefore more expensive.)
4. Is the title unaltered?
5. Are the marks legible on the back?
6. Is the decoration complete?
7. Is it still on its silver chain?

Wine labels

Wine labels were introduced in c.1740 as a way of identifying the new types of wine that were gradually filtering into common circulation. The labels were hung around the neck of the wine bottle from a silver chain and although it is not essential for these to be present, labels without the original chain will be less expensive. There is an almost infinite number of styles available, and a corresponding variety of names, some of which are obscure today (such as "Mountain" and "Vidonia"). Labels made in the 1850s just have the initials, and by the 1860s very few labels were made at all.
*With the exception of Regency wine labels which are cast, most are stamped.
*As well as being made in silver, the labels were also made in electroplate and enamel.

Beware

Check any labels with engraved names carefully for alterations. Common names such as Port have frequently been changed to a rarer and more collectable name by cutting out the original piercing and engraving the new name over the surface.

Collecting

Wine labels bearing obscure names are far more collectable than those with a common name such as Madeira. A premium is paid for a group of labels made by the same maker, but generally labels are collected individually. Labels with common names sell easily and are bought to be used. The rarer ones are bought by collectors and can form a fascinating history of the tastes of late 18thC and 19thC drinkers. The use of labels declined when bottles became properly labelled.

Marks

Early labels have the maker's mark and lion passant. After 1784 many are fully marked. Smaller labels in particular can be incompletely marked.

Sauce labels

Sauce bottle labels in a similar style to wine labels were also produced in the 18thC. These are much smaller than wine labels and were designed to go round the neck of cruet bottles.

This George II silver cartouche-shaped wine label from c.1740 is one the earliest examples made, and few labels pre-date it. These labels were frequently made, as here, by the silversmith Sandylands Drinkwater. The decoration of grape-laden vines did not appear on labels again until the 1820s.
*This label is marked with the maker's mark and lion passant.
*Some guide to dating is provided by the cartouche shape of the label, as this changed in 1760.

Many wine lables were utilitarian with simple borders to make them relatively inexpensive to buy. This label, actually made in 1826 at the height of elaborate taste, is very plain and could have been made at almost any time.

Types and styles

Earlier wine labels were purely functional and tend to have just a plain reeded border. At the beginning of the 19thC labels in the shape of a vine leaf were made, and later in the century grapes and vines with a scroll supported by putti were popular.

Unlike on the previous example, the decoration on the label illustrated below for Madeira is very much in keeping with the highly elaborate styles of the period. This label was made by Rawlings and Summers in 1834

and is a slightly less ornate version of the one in the main picture which has a cast grapevine surround and is centred by Cupids.
*Because this is a particularly common type of wine label and a common name, it is relatively inexpensive.

Regency labels

Wine labels from the Regency period were often cast. They tend to be far more ornate than earlier examples.

Because these silver gilt wine labels have been cast they are significantly heavier than the other examples featured on this page. They are also larger, and were probably designed to be hung on decanters rather than wine bottles. This type was almost exclusively made by silversmiths working for Rundell, Bridge and Rundell – these were made by Paul Storr in 1811.

WINE COOLERS

One of a pair of George III wine coolers; Paul Storr, London; 1809; ht 11½in (29cm); value code A

Identification checklist for an 18th-19thC wine cooler
1. Is the body fully marked?
2. Is the cooler complete with collar and liner?
3. Are the collar and liner part-marked?
4. Does it form one of a pair?
5. Are any decorative motifs elaborate?
6. Has the decoration remained undamaged?

Wine coolers
Although wine coolers were made from the early years of the 18thC, most date from the late 18th and early 19thC. They tend to be of fine quality, and apart from the erasure of coats-of-arms have remained in good condition. Wine coolers were usually made in three parts – body, liner and collar – and were sold as pairs or in larger sets. They invariably had handles because when in use condensation makes them slippery to lift. Many Regency wine coolers were made in silver-gilt which protects the decoration.

Collecting
Wine coolers tend to be very expensive items as they are big and invariably contain a large amount of silver. Elaborate designs and decoration are especially coveted; classical scenes such as those depicted on the example in the main picture were popular. Significant makers include Paul Storr, who made the one above, and other silversmiths working for the leading Regency firm Rundell, Bridge & Rundell. Less elaborate wine coolers were also made in Sheffield plate. You can find a plated cooler without a

collar and liner and although these can be used as flower vases they are significantly less valuable. A single cooler is also much less desirable, worth about a third of the price of a pair.

Marks

The body should be fully marked, usually on the underside; the other pieces should be part-marked in one of two ways:
*with the lion passant, maker's mark, and duty mark (after 1794)
*with a full set of marks apart from the town mark.

This early wine cooler from 1789 is considerably less sought-after than later examples. The plain bucket-shaped body is not cast and is therefore very light and the collar and liner is missing. The lack of a central foot reduces the size – this one is only 8in (20.5cm) high.
*Wine coolers should always be checked for signs of erased arms. Because of the weight of silver used this may be manifested as a dip in the metal rather than a perceptible thinness.

This typical late-Regency wine cooler made by Paul Storr in 1821 has a cast foot which is almost a necessity to support the considerable weight of the cooler, ice and wine. The overhanging border of grapes has been separately cast and applied and is fairly robust. However, the body is not cast and is relatively thin and vulnerable to damage; check that the heavy foot has not pushed into the metal of the body. This liner is made from Sheffield plate – the most expensive wine coolers had silver liners.
*Expect to find a crest on the collar rather than the body on such elaborate pieces as this.

By the early-Victorian period the collar and liner were integrated into one piece as in this pair made by Edward Barnard in 1840. They remained mainly of high quality; this pair is embellished with lavish cast and applied decoration which adds significantly to the weight and value. However, price will be reduced by the presence of the later crest on the side of the body.

A Sheffield Plate entrée dish and cover; c.1830; lgth 14½in (37cm)

Sheffield Plate

Sheffield plate enabled the new merchant classes to buy items which closely resembled silver for a fraction of the cost. Consequently many plated items are domestic wares such as entrée dishes and candlesticks. Plating was introduced in 1742/3 by Thomas Bolsover, a cutler from Sheffield. He is said to have accidentally discovered that melted silver could adhere to copper whilst repairing a knife in his workshop, and soon he was using the process to make a host of affordable items. A silver sheet was placed onto a copper ingot, and all the air removed by hammering. Another layer of copper was applied to protect the silver and the "sandwich" was then placed in a hot fire until the silver melted and fused to the ingot (silver melts before copper). If the ingots were then put through a rolling mill the metal could stretch to an almost infinite length without the silver leaving the copper. Although initially used for small items, the process was soon used for larger items such as entrée dishes and soup tureens. When the plate was rolled out the edges of the sheet would fray, revealing the copper base. To overcome this problem the sheet would be cut at an angle and the top layer of silver folded over to form a rim; later a separate silver edge was applied. A good way to identify Sheffield plate is to run a fingernail underneath the edge. If there is a rim it is Sheffield Plate. Sheffield plate was not really made in any quantity until the 1770s. Up until this time the plate was usually one-sided and the inside of plate items was a dull, tin colour. Items made after 1770 are plated on both sides if necessary. From the 1830s onwards Sheffield plate was also applied to a nickel silver (or German silver) base. This was popular because less silver was required to cover the base metal which was white, and the need for a rollover edge was redundant. Sheffield plate feet and handles are made in two halves which are filled with lead and then soldered together. Not only was this a lengthy and labour intensive process, it was also impractical. This was particularly true in the case of entrée dishes and tureens beause if they were put onto a hot surface the lead solder in the feet would melt and bubble out. On particularly decorative pieces made in the 19thC borders were often struck in thin silver and filled with lead. These were very prone to wear and the lead often shows through on the highlights.

Close plating

Close plating was developed in c.1779 for covering steel. The molten-hot metal was dipped into a mixture of liquid tin, covered with a paper-thin layer of silver foil which was stamped onto the metal with a cloth-covered hammer, and then soldered. It was used particularly for knives, forks and spoons and other small items which were difficult to make from Sheffield plate. Unfortunately the steel base metal rusts when exposed to damp, causing the surface silver to buckle. This is impossible to repair and very few items of close-plated cutlery have survived in reasonable condition today. Candle snuffers are well-suited to close-plating.

Electroplate

A far less expensive and quicker method of manufacture than Sheffield plating is electroplating. No fusion was required and all the handles, feet and finials that previously had to be made in two halves and filled with lead could now be cast in German or nickel silver and then plated in a vat. In addition, borders no longer had to be lead-filled. In little more than a decade the Sheffield plate trade had died out almost completely. It is useful to remember that whereas the surface of Sheffield plate used Sterling Standard (.925), electroplate uses pure silver, which not only gives a whiter, harsher colour, but also provides a useful basis for a chemical test if there is any doubt as to which process has been used.

Electrotyping

Electrotyping enabled copies of complicated items to be produced easily. The technique was perfected by Elkington & Co. in the 1850s. They subsequently took on a Frenchman, L. Morel Ladeuil, to design pieces which they could profitably copy. The process involved the electro-deposition of metal in casts of an object, and then backing the casts with base metal. Accurate multiple copies of pieces such as the charger illustrated on p. 142 could then be produced. It was also useful for producing smaller decorative panels which could be let into sides of large pieces made either in plate or even silver. The process was used to make copies of pieces for reference – Wilfred Cripps arranged for Elkington to copy the Tudor and Jacobean silver in the armoury in the Kremlin in 1885 on behalf of the Victoria and Albert Museum. Electroplate exists in vast quantities and much of it is very well used and not worth buying. Poor plate should be avoided as enough survives in excellent condition to allow would-be buyers to be selective.

SHEFFIELD PLATE 1

A Sheffield plate coffee jug;
c.1790; value code F

Identification checklist for a piece of Sheffield plate
1. Is it made from silver on copper?
2. Is there a silver shield?
3. If it is hollowware is there a seam up the back between the handle sockets?
4. Is there little if any copper visible through the silver?
5. If there is any decoration is it flat-chased?
6. Are any applied borders lead-filled?

Sheffield plate
Plate was introduced in 1742 giving people the chance to buy silver-looking items at affordable prices. Styles correspond to those of silver, although more novelty items were made in plate.

Condition
Condition is very important when buying Sheffield plate. If a piece is worn the copper will show. This is inevitable and although some copper can look attractive, the wear will only get worse, and pieces with large areas of copper showing should be avoided.

Check carefully for any evidence of items being repaired with lead solder, as this will significatnly lower the value.

Sheffield plate feet and handles are made in two halves which are filled with lead and then soldered together. Not only was this a lengthy and labour intensive process, it was also impractical. *If Sheffield plate is damaged it cannot be soldered because as soon as heat is applied to the surface any lead inside will melt.

Decoration

Any decoration on Sheffield plate is usually flat-chased like that on the coffee pot in the main picture. If most Sheffield plate were to be engraved the incision would go right through to the copper which is unsightly. Some early plate has a thicker layer of silver

incorporated into the body so that the decoration could be engraved. In order to decorate a piece of Sheffield plate with a crest or coat-of-arms a pure silver shield would be "rubbed in" to the metal – the surface would be prepared and a silver rectangle or disc fused on tothe body to bear the engraving. This disc can always be seen; if the area is breathed upon a halo around the engraving will be visible (see illustration above).

Entrée dishes

Entrée dishes and their heater bases were often made in silver plate, and many silver examples had plated heater bases to keep the price down (see pp.36-37).

The very elaborate finial on this plated entrée dish from Sheffield, c.1828, has been cast in silver – if it were plate it would have had to be die-stamped and filled.
*The silver finial should be marked with all the relevant silver marks.
*As with any piece of plate that is likely to have been near heat, check the borders carefully for bleeding of the lead, as well as for normal wear.

Although the seam on the body of these candelabra will be disguised, the seam on the sconces should be visible. Check carefully for damage. The branches of candlesticks were often taken off to put away, so check for cracks in the branches, for lead solder repairs and for arms that have bent out. This distinctive pair of 18thC candelabra are in a typical classical style. Plated candelabra branches are often found with silver candlesticks.

SHEFFIELD PLATE 2

The plates above left were made by Matthew Boulton & Co. of Birmingham and can be dated to c.1815 by the coats-of-arms. Plated plates are quite rare because if they were heated the borders (which at this time were filled with lead) would fall off.

Soup tureens

Plated soup tureens are very rare but although expensive, they are still considerably less so than their silver equivalents. The 18thC example above right is a very unusual design and nothing like mainstream silver styles of the time. It will be quite light-weight although the finial, handles and dolphin feet are filled with lead solder. Check these carefully for damage and make sure they are securely attached to the body. Plated tureens from the 19thC are more common.

Engraving

Early Sheffield plate had a heavier deposit of silver than later, which enables the surface to be lightly engraved. In c.1790 less silver was used which led to the need for flat-chasing. Provision for a crest was made by cutting out a patch and letting in a heavily-plated disc. This is normally disguised by a cartouche on the front, and if the back is tinned or double-plated it will not be visible.

This George IV Sheffield plate salver is typical of the period. The arms have been engraved in a rubbed-in silver shield, and the entire surface is flat-chased with blooms and scrolls against a matted ground. Although the quality is good, this type of salver is not particularly sought-after as the decoration is rather excessive. Because the rubbed-in shield is pure silver it tarnishes at a different rate from the rest of the body and will show up clearly. If no disc is visible, the item may have been re-plated at a later date.

Although plated salvers from the 19thC are readiliy available, examples as early as this one made in c.1780 are rare – it can be dated by the beaded border.

This candlestick from c.1780, again in the classical style, preceded the candelabra on the previous page. The body is quite difficult to damage, but check for wear on the leaves wrapped round the columns. The detail is die-stamped and should therefore be crisp. At this time there would be lead in the borders

Marks

Much early Sheffield plate was marked with imitations of silver hallmarks which were surprisingly deceptive at first glance. The Birmingham and Sheffield assay offices opened in 1773 and one of the provisions of opening was that makers of plate should not mark their objects at all.
However, in 1784 the Sheffield office managed to pass a law allowing plate made in Sheffield to be marked with the maker's name or initials, and from this time many marks were registered from this city. Few were from Birmingham.
*An item marked Sheffield Plate on the bottom is modern plate that has been made in Sheffield.

Repair

Avoid any plate items that need repair. Because most borders, feet and handles are lead-filled any solder is likely to start bleeding. Items can be re-plated but this will detract from the value.

Major makers

Makers of Sheffield plate include Joseph Hancock who was instrumental in developing the discovery, and Matthew Boulton who marked his wares with two suns.

Other marks which regularly appear are those of Roberts Cadman & Co. and the crossed keys of either J Parsons & Co. or John Green & Co.

M Boulton & Co.

The premier maker in Birmingham with a large factory operating with 1,000 men by 1764.

John Green & Co.

Successors to J. Parsons & Co. in the early 19thC, and like them specialists in making candlesticks. They took over Parsons' crossed-keys sign.

Thomas Law

An early maker of plate who struck his mark on a piece several times to imitate silver marks.

John Parsons & Co.

Predecessors to J. Green & Co. (see above). They used the crossed-keys mark upside down. The firm included John Winter who specialized in candlesticks.

Roberts, Cadman & Co.

Samuel Roberts and George Cadman started in 1784. Roberts perfected the rubbed-in shield.

Nathaniel Smith & Co.

Registered the hand as a trademark in 1784. Was in partnership with many others until the 1820s.

Henry Wilkinson

Successor to J. Green & Co. Made a huge volume of plate.

ELECTROPLATE 1

An electroplated parcel-gilt sideboard dish; Elkington & Co.;
c.1875, 21¼in (54.5cm) diam; value code D

**Identification checklist for a piece of Elkington
electroplated silver**
1. Is it fine quality?
2. Is the piece marked with the company's date or
alphabet system and the maker's mark?
3. Does it have a PODR number (see p. 185)?
4. Is any gilding in good condition?
5. Is the plating also in good condition?

Electroplate
Sheffield plate virtually
disappeared in the 1840s with the
introduction of electroplating, a
far more efficient and less expensive method of producing silver-
looking goods. Although an electroplated goblet is recorded as
early as 1814, it was not really
until Elkington & Co. took out a
patent for electroplating in 1840
that the process became wide-
spread. The company soon had
control of the market, buying out
their competitors and employing
the best craftsmen.

Method of manufacture
Electroplating involved putting a
metal object in solution in a tank
with a positive wire attached to a
silver anode. A current was then
passed from the positive to the
negative. This resulted in a fine
sheet of silver being applied to
the object, which was whiter and
harsher in appearance than
Sheffield plate. Initially, the base
metal was copper, but later nickel
was used, hence the lettering
EPNS (electroplated nickel silver) which is stamped on many
electroplated wares. Although the
new process was recognized at
once by Sheffield platers as
heralding the end of their indus-
try, it proved a safer means of
gilding. Previously gilding was a
very dangerous process involving
painting an item with gold and
mercury and then burning off the
mercury to leave the gold.

This parcel-gilt electroplated electrotype inkstand made by Elkington, Mason & Co. is based on John Leigton's design for the Commemorative Shield of the Great Exhibition of 1851. A number of these inkstands were made but few have survived in such good condition as this one – the gilding and relief decoration are particularly susceptible to wear. As with the dish in the main picture, condition is crucial.

Marks

Elkington & Co. developed their own system of marking electroplated wears. From 1841 and 1848 they adopted the numbers 1 to 8 for the years, after which they used letters of the alphabet placed in different shields, beginning with the letter K in 1849, and starting the alphabet again in 1865, 1886 and 1912.

The earliest wares were marked "E & Co" crowned in a shield and the word "Electroplate" in three sections.

From 1843 "E M & Co" was added in three sections.

A selection of Elkington & Co.'s makers' marks used by the company on electroplate items.

PODR

In 1842 the PODR system was introduced to register designs with the patent office. The relevant number corresponds to a date before which time the piece should not have been made. The number often appears on plate as many novelty items were made in plate rather than silver.

The fact that this electroplate candlestick has been cast means it could not possibly be Sheffield plate, as these were usually stamped and seamed. As with much electroplate, this candlestick closely follows the style of silver ones of the time (see p. 24).

Condition

Electroplated items are less easily damaged than Sheffield plate as the borders and feet are no longer filled with lead. If damaged they are very rarely worth repairing.

ELECTROPLATE 2

Spoon warmers

A vast amount of spoon warmers were made in electroplate (never in silver). This is a particularly good example because it has

been cast. It also has an internal lip to prevent the spoon from slipping. Because of its fine quality it is worth around six times as much as the more usual type of spoon warmer.

Claret jugs

Claret jugs were made both in solid electroplate or, as here, in glass with plated mounts. Most are fairly utilitarian and these exist in huge numbers today. Elkington & Co. made better-quality examples with parcel-gilt cast motifs and attractively decorated glass bodies.

Check carefully for cracks where the collar is attached to the body. The best way to check for damage is by filling the jug and testing for leaks but unfortunately this is not always possible. Other areas to check are:
*the handle – frequently the handle is inadequate to hold the

weight of the jug. Glass handles crack easily and metal ones are always a better choice, but this one is supported only at the top which means it will be weak – it is better to have a girdle round the centre as well to add strength.
*the spout – broad lips pour well, but narrow ones may drip.
The glass body is rarely plain and is usually engraved or etched. The most decorative jugs tend to be in silver (see pp. 126-127).

Argyles

The argyle was developed towards the end of the 18thC, but only 20thC reproductions were electroplated.

This example has a thick spout which could pour virtually anything, whereas earlier ones were thinner and were designed specifically to pour the juices of meat. The double skinned water jacket on argyles made them a far more effective way of keeping gravy warm than sauce boats, but makes them extremely expensive and difficult to repair.

Collecting

Both Sheffield plate and electroplate are readily available, and any pieces that are in good condition are highly collectable. Early Sheffield plate in particular fetches very high prices. Some large pieces of parcel gilt electroplate, such as centrepieces can be of very fine quality, and if they are in a sought-after style they can fetch almost as high prices as the same items in silver.
*Cased flatware services are also always popular with collectors, provided that they have managed to survive in good condition.

Cruet frames

Cruet frames among the most popular electroplated items. There are two distinct types. The ordinary frames with eight to ten bottles are usually not of very good quality and end to be highly impractical today.

This is an Elkington & Co. electrotype copy of an antique vase made in the mid 19thC by the Danish silversmith, Benjamin Schlick. Schlick, like a number of foreign silversmiths, worked under contract for Elkington & Co. Whereas Morel-Ladeuil who made the charger on p. 142 was with the company for over a quarter of a century, Schlick was only there for a few years in the middle of the 19thC.

Centrepieces

Centrepieces were often electroplated. This example made by Elkington in 1885 is particularly large (31½ in (80cm diam.)) and heavy and is typical of those made in plated silver. Electroplated centrepieces are usually of high quality, and they tend to be expensive – some better examples are parcel gilt and this adds considerably to their value. This type of centrepiece is often found with smaller dessert stands in the same style. *It is very important to check the glass for chips and cracks and to make sure all the parts match. Also make sure that the figures are holding any items they originally had in their hands.

More collectable are frames such as the one illustrated above from c.1860 which had only two or three bottles. These are usually of better quality and tend to have attractive red or blue glass bottles. This particular example is especially desirable because it has plated mounts to the stoppers. The bottles are of wine bottle size. The condition of the glass is crucial to the price of a cruet frame. In addition, any bottles which are made from clear glass need to be well-cut for the frame to be of value today.

AMERICAN SILVER

An early 18thC New England tankard

In the 17thC very few Americans were wealthy, and most of the country's early silverware – English In style – was made for churches. When the Pilgrim Fathers came over to America from Britain on the Mayflower in 1620 they had little money to spend on luxury silver. But they were followed by over 20,000 other settlers, many of whom were political refugees and men of means who brought their own silver out with them. As a result of new trade with these settlers, silver became important in the United States, not only as a symbol of wealth, but also as an asset which provided buying power.

In the colonies Boston was the first major centre of silversmithing, with 24 makers registered between 1650 and 1680. The earliest known piece of marked American silver is a small two-handled dish or wine taster made in Boston in c.1651 by John Hull (1624-83) and Robert Sanderson (1608-93). The following year Hull was appointed to make the shilling, sixpence and threepence coins. He chose as his partner Sanderson, who had previously served a nine year apprenticeship to a London silversmith before emigrating to the United States. Together they produced most of the known early marked examples of silver in the United States, and anything bearing their two names is highly sought-after (only about 40 pieces in total).

Early American silver can be split into two areas of influence – Dutch and English. New York (New Amsterdam until 1664) retained Dutch styles for almost a century after becoming part of the British Colony, and many New York makers have Dutch names. A French influence in New York silver styles came from immigrant Huguenots who fled to America after the Revocation of the Edict of Nantes in 1685. The Dutch influence can be seen in the tall elegant beakers and small teapots made in this area. New York tankards may have a beaded rat tail design down the back of the handle and a band of shallow applied ornament round the base.

English influences prevailed elsewhere in the United States, with Boston and Philadelphia as the main centres of production. Boston was the major sea port and had a flourishing trade which led to a large wealthy population well-catered for by local silversmiths. Philadelphia was the capital, and it saw not only the production by Philip Synge of the inkstand used in the Declaration of Independence, but also a rococo-style kettle by Joseph Richardson which is a rarity not only because very few kettles have survived in the United States, but also because the rococo style rarely appealed to the less exuberant tastes of 18thC America – almost the only other example is a presentation salver made by Lewis Fuetter of New York in the 1770s.

Very little native silver other than the purely utilitarian can be traced in the Southern States, and it seems that most of their silver was imported from Europe. However, imported silver encouraged the raising and maintaining of high standards not only in the south, but also amongst local craftsmen in the north of the country.

American silver candlesticks are rare, which is surprising considering how many early makers produced them – among them John Burt, John Coney and Jeremiah Dummer, who all worked in Boston and were connected with Hull and Sanderson. Despite the fame of the Boston Tea Party, tea caddies are almost unknown in the United States. Oval sugar boxes were more numerous in the United States in the late 17thC than in England, but again they hardly ever appear on the market today.

Neo-classicism was briefly popular in the United States after the War of Independence (1776) and there was a minor flirtation with French Empire styles after the 1812 war. Thereafter, any remaining Puritan tastes vanished to be replaced by astonishingly flamboyant pieces with – as in England at this time – with scarcely a plain surface. The richness and inventiveness of late 19thC American silver is unequalled elsewhere. At the end of the 19thC Tiffany & Co., and Gorham to a lesser extent, produced expensive pieces made of "silver and other metals" in a Art Nouveau style with a strong Japanese influence. These include vases and teapots (see p. 155) which are greatly sought-after today.

Despite 18thC attempts by various centres of production, there was never any centralized assay or marking system in the United States, and the purity of the metal seems to have been taken on trust, guaranteed by the mark of the maker. Generally the standard is Sterling or a little below. Makers marks were simply initials in the beginning, but later on the full surname tended to be used (see p. 153).

A rare American tankard; William Jones, Massachusetts;
1720-1730; ht: 7¾in (19.5cm); value code A

Identification checklist for an early 18thC American tankard from Boston
1. Does it have a slightly domed stepped lid and a cylindrical body?
2. Does the lid have a finial? (A feature particular to Boston tankards.)
3. Is there a girdle? (Not always present.)
4. Is it struck with only a maker's mark?
5. Is the body undecorated?

American tankards
Out of all early American silver it is tankards that appear in the greatest numbers. The example above is typical of New England tankards. New York tankards of the period are quite different with a flatter lid without a finial, a corkscrew thumbpiece and perhaps a small band of applied leafage above the foot. Dutch influences in New York also lead to engraved covers, which were sometimes set with a coin; handles usually ended in a mask, and occasionally had applied decoration at the top.
*On the tankard in the main picture there are heavy indentations on the handle where the thumbpiece has struck it for many years.

This silver tankard was made by Joseph Richardson Sr, in Philadelphia in c.1750. This is early for a baluster shape. It manages to look subtly different to an English equivalent. Tall, cylindrical tankards were popular in the States until the seond half of the 18thC. Richardson was an important Philadelphia maker.

Teapots

The earliest American teapots date from the first quarter of the 18thC and are very rare today.

This New York example from c.1720 shows typical Dutch influences both in the pear-shaped body and the strapwork moulding on the cover. In Boston

and Philadelphia early pots tended to follow the British bullet-shape (see p. 99), but such examples are almost non-existent today.
*As with British examples, early American teapots were small – this particular example is only 6in (15cm) high.

This New York teapot (c.1757) shows the later trend towards higher shapes – this pot is 9in (21cm) tall. Like most early American silver it is typically plain, solid and heavy. British silver at this time usually had a crest or coat-of-arms, but on American examples initials are far more usual (see above). The influence at this time is still Dutch – Dutch teapots of the period were of a very similar style to this but with slightly different proportions.

Teasets

This three-piece teaset was made in Philadelphia in c.1800. The vase-shaped bodies and pedestal bases are typically English in style, but the elongated covers and slightly unusual proportions together with the covered sugar container immediately identify them as American.

AMERICAN SILVER 2

Boston cans
In the United States the British "mug" is known as a "can". The baluster shape was very similar on both sides of the Atlantic, although American examples are a little more bellied. They were

made in reasonable numbers, but this particular can was made in Boston by Paul Revere, the well-known patriot and silversmith, and is therefore very expensive. Famous not only for silver-smithing and political caricatures, Revere also had the time to start a foundry. His most famous piece of silver is the "Soul of Liberty Bowl" made in c.1768, which commemorates the 99 members of the Legislature who refused to withdraw a hostile letter to George III.

Porringers and caudle cups
Porringers and caudle cups were among some of the earliest silver items made in the United States and were used both for domestic and ecclesiastical purposes. What the British call a bleeding bowl (see p. 173), the Americans call a porringer. As many are engraved with the owner's initials they can provide a useful aid to dating silver. The porringer above was made in New York, but they were also made in New England. If turned upside down porringers are very similar to the cover of a skillet (a saucepan raised on three feet) and these may well have provided the inspiration for their manufacture. There is consider-able change over the years in the style and piercing of the handle and this can help to ascertain the date and origin of the porringer.

John Coney
The restrained and elegant shape of the caudle cup below, made by John Coney of Boston in 1690/1710, reflects the British influence of his designs. Coney was probably apprenticed to John Hull of Boston, and his substan-tial output covers the range of Colonial American silver, including a very rare pair of candlesticks. His two main marks included his initials, at first with a fleur-de-lys and then a coney (or rabbit) as a pun on his name.

This rare early saucepan was made by the Dutch-born Myer Myers of New York in 1770 and is characteristically solid and plainly decorated.
*Apart from producing a large and varied ouput of silverware, Myer Myers, a Sephardic Jew, is noted as having made a number of pairs of bells for the Torah scrolls which show distict similarities with an English set made in 1719.

Myer Myers also made this cream jug in c.1745. It is only 4in (10cm) high and is very little different from an English equivalent. However, it is worth considerably more than an English one because of its rarity.

The name of the maker of this 1720s New York silver caster, Henricus Boelen II, confirms the Dutch influence of its style. The proportions of the caster are different from those of English examples. Although the base is the same as an early 18thC English caster, the shape and piercing of the cover are significantly different.
*English casters are found in sets of three from this date, but the American equivalent is rare enough to command a good price even when sold on its own.
*Boelen was one of a number of prominent makers in New York of Dutch and Huguenot rather than British origin. Other makers include van Dyck, Le Roux, and Onclebagh.

Despite being made by a large range of 17thC craftsmen in the United States, and their obvious necessity, American candlesticks are extremly rare until the early 19thC. Consequently this example will command a premium

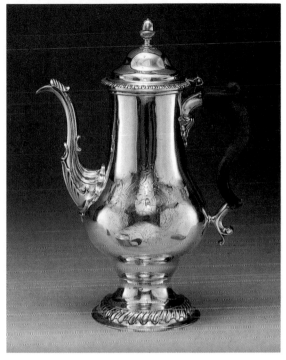

An American silver coffee pot; Philadelphia; c.1765; value code C.

Identification checklist for a mid-18thC American coffee pot
1. Is the body plain? (Rococo influences were never popular in the United States.)
2. Is the pot marked?
3. Does it stand on a raised central foot?
4. Is the pot engraved with initials rather than a coat-of-arms?
5. Are any decorative borders simple?

Coffee pots
Early American coffee pots are not as common as American chocolate pots, which were made in a very similar shape but with a hole in the cover enabling the sediment to be stirred by a rod. Early teapots are also rare, the first ones originating in New York with Dutch or Huguenot influences as might be expected from the names of the makers.

Coffee pots were made individually rather than in sets until the end of the 18thC. The pot in the main picture has a distinctive gallery cover and beaded decoration. The elongated shape of this pot continued into the early 19thC with the vase-shaped bodies which have much longer necks than their English equivalents. Later pots were profusely chased with floral motifs.

Cake baskets

This cake basket was made in New York in c.1792 by Voorkis & Schanck. With its elegant outline and pierced decoration it is almost identical to English and Dutch examples of the period. The piece shows that even a century after the Dutch lost possession of New York, they were still the pre-eminent silversmiths.

Because far fewer baskets were made in the United States than in Britain, this one would be far more expensive than a British one. The pretty naturalistic bright-cut engraving makes this basket particularly desirable, as very little American silver was engraved, possibly because of a lack of skilled craftsmen.

Makers marks

There was never any central control over the marking of silver and as a result marking was done on a local basis. For many years silver was struck with just the name of the maker. In New Amsterdam, and New York after 1664, the makers often struck their mark in a heart-shaped cartouche; in New England simple initials were used. Later on names were stamped in full. The lack of control over makers extended to the purity of silver used. As an English colony, the early makers generally used the Sterling Standard (.925), but this was less adhered to in the 19thC when much mid-century silver was stamped "D" or "C" or with the words "coin" or "dollar" in full as an indication of origin. This was .900 standard. "Sterling" is struck on later products as an indication of higher quality and is still in use today. Only in Baltimore in 1814 was any formal attempt made to open an assay office.

Lewis Fueter (c.1770-1775)

New York maker of one of the very few pieces of American rococo silver ever made.

Gorham Manufacturing Co. (1818-present day)

Founded by Jabez Gorham in Providence, Rhode Island. Joined T. J. Pairpont in 1868 and began marking their products with both a date and trade mark.

Samuel Kirk (1793-1872)

A major manufacturer from Baltimore of every type of silver. His business developed on a huge scale.

Myer Myers (1723-1795)

Philadelphia maker of a large amount of good-quality American silver.

Paul Revere jnr (1735-1818)

Prolific maker of silver but also famous for his role in the American War of Independence.

Tiffany & Co. (1837-present day)

Founded by Charles Louis Tiffany. Opened a branch in Paris in 1853.

AMERICAN ART SILVER

Towards the end of the 19thC American silver had begun to adopt its own style. Production was largely led by Tiffany & Co., founded in New York in 1834, and Gorham & Co., founded in Providence, Rhode Island, in 1831. Their silverware displays a strong oriental influence, particularly that of Japan. Many pieces are in the Art Nouveau style popular in Britain and Europe at this time, and incorporate stylized flowers and fruit into the decoration. Decoration also sometimes took its inspiration from the use of the object it was adorning. For example, Gorham& Co. made ice bowls shaped as blocks of ice with polar bear handles.

This pair of candelabra was made by Tiffany & Co. in c.1885 in the popular Chrysanthemum pattern which is applied to a host of other American silver, including a flatware service. Foliage decoration is typical on late-19thC silver. Although there are many 19thC candlesticks there are very few early examples. This pair are heavy – 373oz (10dwt) – and of typically high quality.

These claret jugs made by Gorham in 1890 represent the height of American over-embellishment on silver. They were hand-made, and records report that they took over 44 hours to turn and a further 50 hours to chase. Today's relatively low price does not reflect the great amount of skill and imagination neded to make them, as contemporary demand for simpler fashions have caused the value of such decorative items to fall in recent years.

The American preference for naturalistic and Japanese motifs is evident in this parcel-gilt engraved fish slice made by Gorham & Co. in c.1880. It is very decorative and the intricacy of the design is unmatched in Europe.There is a huge variety of different sized spoons and forks in a large American service.

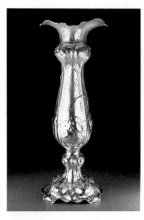

Between 1891 and 1910 Gorham & Co. produced a range of hand-made "martelé" silverware in Britannia standard which now constitutes some of the most collectable Art Nouveau silver around. The lightly-chased decoration and fluid form of this vase made in 1905 is typical of their martelé wares – the flowers are a common Art Nouveau motif. Although the higher standard of metal is noticealy softer than other types, and wears more quickly, it is also much easier to work. This factor must have outweighed the disadvantages of using a pure metal in making these martelé wares. This style, also used by the firm to make a number of claret jugs, is not as popular as that of their mixed metal pieces, which had a Japanese influence that made them appealing to a far wider public.

*Much martelé ware was made on a massive scale – at one point the firm made a martelé dressing table and stool for an exhibition to publicize the skills of their craftsmen and the marketing skills of themsevles.

"Sterling silver and other metals" – Tiffany & Gorham

Tiffany & Co. produced a number of items made of silver and other metals which are clearly marked "sterling silver and other metals". In England such items could not be hallmarked as a hallmark suggests it is silver. These mixed metal pieces tend to be very expensive. Many of them are decorative, but utilitarian wares such as tea sets and tea trays were also made. Gorham & Co. produced a number of similar wares.

Tiffany produced the mixed metals vase on the right in c.1880. The copper ground has been applied with sprays of silver flowers and a brass bamboo plant. The motifs of dragonflies, snails and flowers are typical of the Art Nouveau movement. Like all similar pieces it is stamped "Sterling Silver and Other metals".

This silver and other metals Japanese-style teapot was made by Tiffany & Co. in c.1880. The decoration of trailing vines leaves, butterflies and a dragonfly is typically naturalistic and is redolent of the Art Nouveau style in Britain. This type of work has a unique sculptural quality and finish.

MISCELLANEOUS

A cow creamer; John Schuppe; c.1760

The earliest silver was often bought for display purposes, and as a ready source of money if needed. Bills for early silver came in two parts of more or less equal proportion for a simple piece. Half the bill was for the metal and the other half for the "fashion" (ie. the cost of making it up). This system changed in the early 18thC with the rise to prominence of a large merchant class and the introduction of steam-powered rolling mills which together increased the number of potential buyers and reduced manufacturing costs. The early 19thC invention of spinning metal over a chuck on a lathe further reduced mass-production costs and, coupled with stamping and the use of dies, this revolutionized silver production techniques. Grand pieces of display silver remained expensive, but otherwise there was a huge upsurge in the production of domestic silver at lower prices, and for those who could not afford silver, plated silver.

In the 18thC this led, with a few exceptions, to a loss of imagination and to mainly reproductions of what had been produced before in earlier centuries. This was compensated for as far as the collector is concerned by a broader range of items to buy. These included among other things, photograph frames, brushes, boxes of all sorts and sizes, pin cushions and card cases. Larger pieces, and silver given as prizes and presentations in an unprecedented fashion, was decorated with more easily applied fancy stamping which suited the lavish tastes of the period.

There is a vast amount of small or unusual items made in silver which today can be collected by people with even the most modest budget. Frequently such pieces have been produced in areas away from London, in among other places, Birmingham, Leeds, Cork, Dublin and Scotland. A number of others were made on the Continent, particularly in Germany, where a number of parcel gilt novelties were produced and then exported for sale in Britain. Many of these novelty items date from the Victorian period onwards, when production costs were far lower. A lot of them were figural – for example silver-mounted claret jug, inkwells and even candlesticks were made in the shape of numerous animals such as bears and dogs. The type, size and variety of boxes made for tobacco, snuff, smelling salts and numerous other substances is so expansive that the collecting of boxes has formed a whole new collecting area. Most are highly decorative and, because they are small, they are affordable.

Irish silver has many similarities to English silver of the period. Even in the 18thC many pieces were chased, and this tradition continued into the 19thC. Some silver produced for the domestic market is larger than its English equivalent, perhaps because Irish families were usually far bigger – coffee pots are a good example of the discrepancy in size. One Irish peculiarity is the dish ring, made from the middle of the 18thC onwards to hold hot dishes at the table; others include the potato ring; and late 18thC flatware made in Dublin, Cork and Limerick which had engraved pointed handles. Harp-handled cups are also typically Irish, as are butter dishes of the early 19thC.

Civil and religious strife in Scotland caused much of their old silver to be destroyed, and as elsewhere in Britain little secular silver from Scotland has survived from before the Restoration in 1660. Even more so than in Ireland, there are numerous small towns where silver was marked. However, the majority of Scottish silver that comes on the market today is flatware, often made in the Fiddle pattern, and distinctive from the English equivalent by its particularly long "fiddle". Quaiches, used for sharing whisky around a table are obviously Scottish in origin; these attractive thistle-shaped cups were mainly made in Edinburgh.

A number of minor guilds in England produced silver until the Act of 1697 prevented them from hallmarking their own wares. Most of the silver that survives from these guilds are spoons, an area where much current research is being carried out. A very small amount of domestic plate made in Leeds and Hull has also survived. The anchor town mark of Birmingham frequently appears on a vast array of boxes produced in the 18thC onwards as the town produced small silver items in their thousands. Old spoons are widely collected. The price of Apostle spoons depends very much on a combination of condition and date – 16thC examples are much more desirable than later ones and anything before the reign of Elizabeth I is now very rare indeed. Out of all areas of silver collecting, this is probably the most specialist, and considerable detailed knowledge is needed to buy wisely. However, many 17thC Apostle spoons are relatively inexpensive, and for most collectors they are the only piece of affordable secular silver they can buy that dates from before the Restoration in 1660.

INKSTANDS

A silver inkstand; William Cripps;
1749; value code B

Identification checklist for an 18thC inkstand
1. Is it marked in a line underneath the tray?
2. Are all of the bottles and the bell also marked by the same maker?
3. Is there a dip in the tray to prevent the pen from rolling around?
4. Do the borders of the bottles and bells match the border on the inkstand?
5. Are the tops of the bottles part-marked?
6. Is any crest or coat-of-arms original?
7. Is there no evidence of damage to the piercing on the pounce pot?
8. Is the method of securing the bottles intact?

Inkstands
Early 17thC inkstands were rectangular and large, with hinged lids, but these were soon replaced by a stand with three or four bottles – one for ink, one for sand or "pounce", one for sealing wafers, and a final one for cleaning shot (to clean the pen nib). By the 1740s the number of bottles tended to be only two – for ink and sand – and there was now a bell in the middle so that the letter writer could call a servant to take the letter away.
*Treasury inkstands – oblong two-compartment stands with a central divide – have been made since the 17thC. They are large and plain and usually of a good weight with a large surface area for a presentation inscription to be engraved.
*Pounce – powdered cuttlefish bone – was dusted over the ink instead of using blotting paper.

Collecting
Inkstands are highly collectable because they make very handsome presents and are small, interesting items which can be displayed well on a writing desk. They have come to be viewed somewhat as a status symbol and tend to be expensive.

Marks
Early inkstands are marked in a line underneath the tray, with the bottles and bell fully marked and the tops part-marked.

Beware
Because bells are desirable in their own right they were often separated from the rest of the inkstand and sold individually. Replacement bells on inkstands tend not to be marked. Any inkstand which has its original bell is much more desirable, but today is something of a rarity.

By the middle of the 18thC ink-stands had glass bottles. This example was made by William Plummer in 1767. The bottles have silver collars and detachable silver tops which should all be part-marked to match the rest of the stand – any replacements will reduce the value. The detachable silver cages to hold the bottles should also be marked with the maker's mark and lion passant. Check that the bottles match and are the same size and that there is no damage – sometimes the tops rattle loosely because the collars are missing. Also check the pierc-ing on the feet for damage. Although this example is very large – 14½in (36.5cm) long – and heavy – 57 oz (14dwt) – many were lightweight and should be examined carefully.

This inkstand was made in 1814 by the well-known makers, John and Thomas Settle of Sheffield. Although fairly typical for the time, this one is a little simpler and lighter than comparable London examples and would have been less expensive. The stand now has a taper stick to melt the sealing wax, and this forms the lid of the wafer box. Sometimes these are sold on their own as miniature taper sticks, but they will only be part-marked and will have a locating ring which was used to hold them on to the wafer box. The two bottles are for different colour inks. The border on this example is known as

"tongue and dart" – check that all the borders match and that each individual item is marked. John and Thomas Settle were also well-known makers of Sheffield plate from the 1770s.

An alternative style of inkstand produced at the end of the 18thC is this one made by John Robbins in 1800. The cover opens to reveal the contents inside – a pen, inkwell, wafer box, pounce pot, sealing wax holder and even an ivory tablet for making notes on! The globe has to be a reason-able size to hold all the separate parts – this example is 8in (22cm) high. However, these stands tend not to have been particularly robust, and pieces are frequently missing or damaged. They were not a very popular design and were only in circulation for a short time.
*All the separate parts should be marked, although it would be hard to mark the sealing wax holder without flattening it
*From 1800 fragile items were exempt from being marked.

159

BOXES 1

A silver nutmeg grater;
c.1685; lgth 2in (5.5cm); value code F

***Boxes come in a wide range of shapes and sizes with a
variety of uses. Among the most collectable are nutmeg
graters, snuff boxes, vinaigrettes and freedom boxes.
Other desirable boxes are those for visiting cards.**

Nutmeg graters
Made only in the late 17thC,
these very small boxes – usually
between 1in (2.54cm) and 2in
(5.8cm) in diameter – have a
hinged lid and base and a
compartment to hold the whole
nutmeg. Inside there is a grater
grille. Usually the boxes are tear-
drop shaped as in the example in
the main picture or they have a
domed lid – to accommodate the
oval-shaped spice. The nutmeg
grater in the main picture is
typically decorated with a flower
head; other examples are
engraved with leafage.
*Nutmeg graters are a popular
collecting area and because they
are relatively uncommon they
tend to be relatively expensive.
*As with most nutmeg graters of
the period, this box bears only
the maker's mark.
*Check that the hinge is not
loose and that the grille is
undamaged.

Makers
Silver boxes were produced by
specialist makers – perhaps the
most famous is Nathaniel Mills of
Birmingham.

Tobacco boxes
Tobacco boxes were made from
the late 17thC to the early 18thC.
At first they were oval with a
detachable cover which rules out
any idea of their use for snuff.

This tobacco box made by
Edward Cornock in London in
1715 is a typical example. The lid
is not hinged but detachable and
it should be part-marked to
match the base, which is marked
on the inside. These boxes are
frequently decorated with an
elaborate coat-of-arms such as the
one seen here, but are otherwise
plain. Once again tobacco boxes
are rare. Price will depend greatly
on the quality of the engraving.

Snuff boxes and mulls

Silver snuff boxes to hold ready-grated snuff were made from the second quarter of the 18thC onwards, at the time that the tobacco box fell from use.

The shape of this pair of early snuff mulls from c.1745 is typically Scottish. The ivory and ebony bands are unusual, but even those with silver sides are often inlaid with other materials. This type of snuff mull tends to be very decorative and the subject presents enormous scope for the collector. They are not usually marked.

This type of snuff box made in the middle of the 18thC was mounted either with a cowrie shell or, as with this example, the shell of a tortoise. Cowrie shell boxes are particularly vulnerable to damage so check that the shell has not cracked or been repaired. These are quite popular with collectors and can be found either marked or unmarked – marked ones command a premium. Price is also determined by the attractiveness of the box.

Later snuff boxes such as this one from 1827 tend to be larger and heavier than earlier boxes. The cast decoration of a hunting scene seen here was particularly popular – other subjects were shooting, drunken carousing and classical themes. A premium is paid for a box depicting a particularly sought-after pastime – golfing scenes are extremely desirable.

*Decoration is cast and chased and the value depends greatly on the condition. A box with worn details or where the pattern on the base has rubbed as a result of being pulled along a table will be worth considerably less than one in good condition.

*Hinges are almost impossible to repair as if heat is applied to the metal it may distort.

In the Victorian times engraved snuff boxes were popular and hunting scenes still featured strongly. The engraving should be in good condition and of good quality – any wear will reduce the value of the box considerably. Many Victorian boxes were presented as gifts and sometimes have lengthy inscriptions on the inside. Although inscriptions can greatly devalue the price of large display items such as sauce tureens, because in this case the inscription is on the inside of the box it will not greatly affect the value unless it has been added at a later date.

Boxes of the 1880s sometimes echoed those of the 1730s with similar octagonal shapes and engraving – only the construction of the hinges will be different. This example made in 1881 is engraved with a classical profile within a formal foliate background. Quality is usually high.

BOXES 2

Vinaigrettes

Vinaigrettes were first made towards the end of the 18thC and continued to be produced until the middle of the 19thC. Designed to be carried in a waistcoat pocket, they are significantly smaller than snuff boxes. Inside there is a pierced hinged silver grille, possibly still holding a piece of old sponge underneath which would have originally been soaked in smelling salts. Earlier vinaigrettes are very simple with crudely pierced grilles, whereas later ones have elaborate piercing. Most of them are rectangular, but they come in an infinite variety. The inside is always gilded – if not the box has been altered or repaired.

*Check that a small snuff box is not a vinaigrette with the grille missing – even if there is no trace of a hinge there will be a thumb indentation under the lid.

*The grille prevents the sponge from falling out and allows the smell of the salts to filter through. Sometimes, particularly on early, circular examples, the grille is not hinged but simply wedged and it can easily be lost.

of its associations with the novelist Sir Walter Scott; as is Newstead Abbey, home of the poet Lord Byron.

Numerous vinaigrettes were made in the shape of purses. At 1in (2.9cm) diameter, these are particularly small – "castle-topped vinaigrettes" are 1¾in (4.5cm) wide. This particular example was made in Birmingham in 1835.

Marks

Vinaigrettes were almost invariably made in Birmingham. They are marked inside on the base, on the cover and also on the grille.

Card cases

Most card cases were made in Birmingham. Used to hold visiting cards, they are larger than vinaigrettes – around 4in (10cm) – and are flat to fit inside a pocket. Decoration can be die-struck and similar to that on "castle-topped" vinaigrettes, but usually it is less elaborate, with simple engraved borders.

Vinaigrettes can be engraved, cast, chased, or as in the case of these examples, die-stamped with scenes of well known private houses, cathedrals and monuments. The range is vast, but some subjects are rarer than others and these will command the highest prices. Windsor Castle is very common; Abbotsford is desirable because

This card case made in Birmingham in 1858 is one of the more decorative examples with an elaborate border and a die-

struck image of Cork Castle in the centre. Because the cases were constantly being taken out of a pocket high relief decoration such as on this example is susceptible to wear.
*Card cases do not tend to have the same popular appeal as vinaigrettes.

Damage
Card cases are stamped in two halves. Frequent use can cause the seam to split and this is impossible to repair.

Freedom boxes
Freedom boxes were presented to a person together with the freedom of a town or city and are engraved with the corresponding arms of the city on one side and an inscription to the bearer on the other. If the recipient was a particular friend a gold freedom box would be given.
*In the Regency period a number of people (including the Duke of Rutland) melted these freedom boxes down and made them into salvers, engraving the coats-of-arms of the various corporations on the front.

This freedom box is marked with the maker's mark only – William Reynolds of Cork. Irish provincial examples such as this are particularly collectable. Freedom boxes are all a standard size of about 2¾in (7cm) diameter.
*Very few freedom boxes have retained any original documents.

Vesta boxes
Vesta boxes made to hold matches have become increasingly more collectable over recent years. Dating from c.1880 onwards, they were made in a wide variety of shapes and sizes.

Any unusual item of silver will comman a premium. This vesta case has a hinged lid at one end and a wheel which could be turned to move the wick – a very rare feature.

Another novelty piece from the late 19thC, this example shows how any shape was used for vesta cases. This one is made from a base metal (brass) but will still command a premium price. Base metals were often used in an imaginative way to make less expensive items.

Tobacco rasps
This tobacco rasp was made by Thomas Meriton in London, 1810. Also known as a snuff grater, these boxes were made in the late 18thC with scroll handles to enable the box to be hung on the wall.

APOSTLE SPOONS

A Henry VIII silver Apostle spoon; London; 1528; lgth 7in (17.7cm), value code B

Identification for a 16thC London Apostle spoon
1. Is the bowl marked with the leopard's head?
2. Are the rest of the marks stamped along the back of the handle?
3. Is the Apostle clearly recognizable?
4. Is the nimbus (halo) still present?
5. Is the Apostle joined to the stem with a "V" joint? (Provincial spoons have a lap joint.)

Apostle spoons
Apostle spoons first appeared during the reign of Henry VIII and for many they were the only item of silver they had. They were made in huge numbers both in London and in the provinces. They are so-named because the finials are headed by apostles and

saints, each one identifiable by the emblem he carries (see opposite). Very few full sets survive – only four sets of 12 and four of 13 have ever been recorded. Sets comprise the 12 apostles and Christ as The Master, or The Master and 11 apostles. They should all be made by the same maker in the same year. Production of London apostle spoons stopped in the reign of Charles I, but provincial ones were made for another 20 years.

Marks

London Apostle spoons are marked with the leopard's head in the bowl and the other marks along the back. Provincial ones sometimes have the town mark in the bowl and others on the back of the stem. Early spoons are marked further towards the bowl than later examples.

Fakes

Because Apostle spoons are so expensive attempts are often made to transform other types of spoons into Apostle spoons by cutting off the stem half way up and attaching an apostle to the end. As long as the collector is aware of this type of alteration they are easy to detect, but unsuspecting buyers can be fooled.

Collecting

Apostle spoons are usually bought singly. Price depends upon a combination of age and the state of wear, assuming the spoons are of equal quality. The Master always commands the highest prices. Otherwise there is no particular preference, but spoons where it is obvious who the saint is are more desirable than those where they are difficult to identify. The oldest examples are the rarest today.

The Symons set of Apostle spoons shown below is exceptional in that it is complete and in very good condition.

Identifying the Apostles

It is possible to recognize the individual Apostles by the emblems they hold in their right hand, although sometimes these may be very difficult to discern that easily.

left to right, top to bottom:
St Matthias, St James the Greater, St Jude,
St Matthew, St Andrew, St Simon, St Thomas,
St John, St Peter, St James the Less,
St Philip and St Bartholomew.

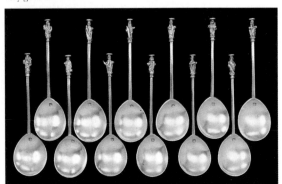

MISCELLANEOUS DRINKING VESSELS

A stirrup cup; Smith and Sharp;
1787; lgth 5¼in (13.5cm); value code C

*There were many types of drinking vessel in silver which do not fit into any of the other categories in this book.

Stirrup cups

Stirrup cups were used for drinking a toast at hunts, and by the nature of their shape they could not be put down until the vessel was empty. They were first made in the 1770s and continued to be produced throughout the century. Most common are those in the shape of fox masks; others are in the shape of greyhounds. The earliest stirrup cups tend to have longer noses and are more stylised than those from the reign of George IV which are shorter and more textured. Later stirrup cups can be cast making them much heavier than late 18thC examples which are normally raised or stamped. With a few expensive exceptions stirrup cups were seldom made in silver-gilt.

Any stirrup cup which can be traced to an exact hunt is particularly desirable. The stirrup cup featured in the main picture above has an engraved vignette of a hunting scene underneath the chin which gives it added charm; others are inscribed around the collar with details of the hunt.

Marks

Stirrup cups were marked in a line around the neck and the marks are frequently difficult to discern within the decorative chasing.

This later stirrup cup made by Paul Storr in 1822 was given as a prize at the Mostyn Hunt Races, and bears an inscription to this effect around the collar. Expensive examples like this were usually gilded. Sometimes stirrup cups were gilded at a later date, so check that the details are not worn underneath as this suggests later gilding.

20thC stirrup cups

Throughout the 20thC stirrup cups have been produced in a wide variety of shapes, from rabbits' heads to horses' heads. These examples are cast and are usually of high quality. They are particularly popular with collectors if they come in pairs or larger sets.

Quaiches

Quaiches originated in Scotland and therefore are particularly popular with Scottish collectors. They were filled with whisky and passed round the table to share. They vary little in design and can be quite small – 4in (10cm) diam. including handles – and solid.

This quaiche was made in 1700, possibly in Edinburgh. Other examples were wooden and had silver mounts. This example has been engraved to simulate wood.
*Early quaiches, unmarked or with the makers's mark only, tend to be larger than later examples which sometimes served as communion cups in the way that beakers and occasionally tankards were in the United States. The handles are initialled rather than the body.

Novelty claret jugs

During the Victorian period novelty claret jugs were produced in the shape of birds, animals and fish. These are rare today and very popular with collectors and even a simple one is worth several thousand pounds.
*The more unusual the subject of the jug, the greater its popularity with the collector.

This jug made by Crichton Brothers in 1885 is particularly fine. The condition of the glass is crucial as it is impossible to replace. Sometimes the glass is frosted, as here, and at other times it is clear. Each separate piece of silver should be marked. Because the jugs have always been prized they tend to have survived in good condition.

Neffs

Neffs are ship-shaped. They were made throughout Europe, particularly in the 19thC. They come apart below the line of cannon and some can be used to hold a bottle at the dining table. Many were exported to Britain and these should bear English import marks – any that do not are worth far less because they are likely to be below Sterling Standard and therefore cannot legally be described as silver. Value depends greatly on size, condition, and to a certain extent, cleanliness. Most imports came from Germany and Holland.

Neffs are exceptionally difficult to clean and it is advisable to have them sprayed with a tarnish-proof coating for protection. This example is particularly large at 2ft (61cm) long, and is worth a substantial amount of money. Smaller lighter versions can be as little as a tenth of the value of this one. Those in good condition are particularly sought-after.
*Before buying, check carefully that there is no damage to any of the masts and fine details.

Two George III silver soup ladles. Left: Limerick; Patrick Connell; c.1780; Right: London, Edward Wakelin; 1751

*Numerous extra pieces of silver flatware were made which do not form part of a service, but which can be matched up with one if necessary.

Ladles

Silver soup ladles were introduced at the time of soup tureens in the 1740s. Styles tend to follow those of other flatware of the period (see pp. 60-65), but a few highly elaborate examples were made. Soup ladles were sold singly, but sauce ladles, made in the same style, came in pairs. Circular bowls are more desirable.

Irish ladles

The fact that the soup ladle shown above left was made in Limerick increases its value considerably. Further features which add to its desirability are:
*shell bowl
*bright-cut engraving on the handle
*original crest.

Decoration

The decoration on the handle is typical of pieces made in Cork and Limerick at this time.
*Check a crest has not been removed, and for splits in the bowl and cracks in the handle.

Fish slices

Early fish slices had turned wooden handles but by the 19thC when many slices formed part of a service they were replaced by silver handles. From the mid-19thC onwards fish slices were made with a matching fork and were called fish servers.
*It is debatable whether early slices were made for serving fish or gateau. Later ones were often engraved with fish which revealed their original use.

This Dublin fish slice from 1758 is one of the earliest examples made. All slices tend to follow a standard shape and any inventiveness is in the pierced decoration – some Victorian ones were particularly innovative. So-called spoon-handled fish slices are much less desirable and have broad scimitar-shaped blades with simple piercing. Later Victorian ones can have loaded handles which need careful checking for splits.

Condition
Fish slices are highly susceptible to damage, especially where the handle joins the slice. Sometimes the handle is replaced with one from a completely different period and this is particularly undesirable.
*Check for wear to the marks.

Spoon trays
In the early 18thC tea was drunk from a bowl which did not have a saucer and silver spoon trays were provided to rest the teaspoon on. When cups and saucers were introduced later in the 18thC production died out. Spoon trays can be distinguished from snuffer trays by their absence of a handle (see pp. 44-45), but occasionally they are described as pen trays.

Only made for a short time they are a historical curiosity popular with collectors today.

This spoon tray from 1717 is absolutely typical of those produced, with its oval shape, fluted decoration and absence of feet. In the centre is an entwined monogram.
*Spoon trays should be marked in each corner.

Serving spoons
Serving spoons are larger than table spoons and were used for serving soup until the end of the 19thC when the soup spoon was introduced. They were produced in the same patterns as services and are most collectable as pairs although single ones are also acceptable.
*As with any other silver spoon make sure that the tip of the bowl is not worn as this will considerably reduce the value.

Marrow scoops
Marrow scoops were made in enormous quantities from the 17thC onwards to scoop out bone marrow, a great delicacy at the time. The scoops are all the same size with a large and a small end to cater for different bones. They are marked in the centre on the back. They are always plain, although occasionally there is a crest on the wider end. Even

though there are considerable numbers around there is a high demand for them.

Most scoops were made in the mid- to late 18thC and this example from the reign of Queen Anne is very rare and consequently very expensive. As with other types of flatware of the period marrow scoops have often had their marks folded in which makes them impossible to read.

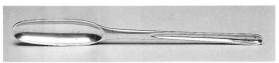

ADDITIONAL TABLEWARE 2

Apple corer

Apple corers were made from the end of the 17thC, but the majority date from the end of the 18thC to the beginning of the 19thC. They are relatively rare and are of little use today because they are no longer large enough for apples, which are now bigger. However, they are popular with collectors because of their novelty value.

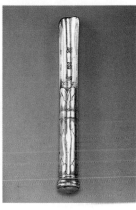

This unusually early (17thC) corer is very similar to later ones. Corers are usually marked in the blade – this one is marked with the maker's mark only, repeated several times. Condition is usually reasonable because corers were not regularly used.

Mote spoons

Mote spoons were used to skim the tea leaves off the surface of tea. They were an 18thC invention and most of them were made in the middle years of the century. Later ones had increasingly elaborate pierced bowls. The mote spoon below second

left, made by Isaac Callard in c.1740, has a typically decorative pierced bowl. Any further decorative features, such as applied shell work, will increase the price. Some attempts have been made

Sugar tongs

Most late 18thC sugar tongs are very simple but by the middle of the 19thC designs tended to be more imaginative.

This pair of tongs was made by Francis Higgins, a prolific maker of fancy flatware. Attractive features include the gilt tube handle and the Blackamoor finial. These later tongs tend to be in good condition, but early plain examples which have a simple loop handle are more fragile and should be checked at the arch for breakages or cracks. Early tongs are available in vast numbers and are usually of poor quality and consequently are among the least expensive pieces of silver. However, examples such as this can be worth significantly more.

to convert teaspoons into mote spoons because mote spoons are far more valuable than teaspoons. However, the bowls of teaspoons are larger and teaspoons do not have the point on the end of the handle which is found on mote spoons (this was used to poke down the spout of the teapot to unblock the neck).

*Mote spoons are usually marked quite close to the bowl with the lion passant and the maker's mark, and the date is usually ascertained from the style of the spoon.

*Some mote spoons have attractive scrolls or other motifs struck on the back of the bowl which will increase the value.

Caddy spoons

Caddy spoons were introduced when tea caddies no longer had a cap which could be used as a measure for the tea (see p.109). They were made in vast quantities from the last quarter of the 18thC, mostly in Birmingham by the same smallworkers who made boxes and wine labels. They are made from sheet or die-cast silver, and this means they are quite fragile, so check that there are no splits in the bowl or damage to the handle. They are highly collectable because there is such a range of designs and prices – 19thC examples with simple bright-cut handles and plain bowls are worth only a few pounds each, but more elaborate designs can be worth hundreds of pounds. Any damaged ones should be avoided.

Caddy spoons were produced in an infinite variety of designs, and any which are unusual or rare are particularly collectable, especially examples in the shape of a jockey cap or eagle's wing – the leaf design of this spoon is quite popular.

*Jockey cap caddy spoons have been made out of the back of watches, by adding a peak to the bowl. However these can easily be identified because watches are marked in a middle in a group whereas caddy spoons are marked in a line on the peak.

Grape scissors

Grape scissors were used to cut off the grapes from a bunch, but they never worked effectively despite the fact that they had a steel insert in the blade. However, they are highly sought-after as they make ideal gifts, and they command high prices. They can come either as part of a dessert set with two pairs of picks and two pairs of nutcrackers, or on their own. Examples still in their fitted cases are particularly desirable. Early scissors from the late 18thC are elegant and fairly simple; later Regency and Victorian ones are very elaborate and imaginatively decorated.

Some of the more expensive grape scissors, such as this Victorian pair made by Elkington in 1890, are parcel gilt. A vast number were also made in plate. Price depends very much on quality and maker – a standard good-quality pair are worth a few hundred pounds, but an elaborate Regency pair by Paul Storr could be worth thousands of pounds.

Asparagus tongs

Asparagus tongs are shaped like a giant pair of sugar tongs. They were usually bright-cut engraved at the end of the 18thC. In the 19thC the grips broaden and are pierced and the handles start to match services.

MISCELLANEOUS DISHES, BOWLS AND BOTTLES

A 20thC Irish dish ring;
value code E/F

*Dish rings were made exclusively in Ireland from the middle of the 18thC onwards. The best examples are decorated with lively scenes of farm animals and rustics and have a skillfully engraved coat-of-arms set within a large cartouche.

Dish rings

The dish ring in the main picture above dates from the early years of the 20thC when relatively large numbers were made. The stamped decoration is rather coarse but still check carefully for any damage. Because the Irish hallmarking system was haphazard in the mid 18thC, dish rings can be incompletely marked. Ideally, they should be marked in a line on the rim. Rare and expensive, Irish provincial examples command substantially higher prices than those made in Dublin. Modern dish rings are far less desirable and are worth only a quarter of the price of an 18thC example. The rings are sometimes fitted with a blue glass liner to hold fruit or flowers. Because dish rings are attractive and were pierced in a variety of designs they are a popular collecting area.

Dish crosses

Dish crosses were made between 1740 and 1770 and were designed for keeping the dishes warm at the dining table. They are quite rare but because they do not have much aesthetic appeal they are relatively inexpensive.

This dish cross has a central burner to keep the dish warm. The angle and length of the legs can be adjusted for different-sized dishes and the mechanism is susceptible to damage.
*Dish crosses should be marked under the burner and all the separate pieces should have a mark.
*Dish crosses are sometimes called potato rings, but it is hard to see how this could be correct. They probably held a pile of plates of a similar size, or a bowl.

Cheese dishes
Cheese dishes were made in relatively small numbers for wealthy households at the end of the 18thC and the beginning of the 19thC. Although they are neither particularly decorative nor useful they are rare and demand for them is quite high.

This cheese dish, made by William Stephenson of London in 1789, is a typical example, with its rectangular shape and wooden handle which screws into the body. The lid is held at an angle of 45 degrees by a chain which is attached to the handle. When the dish is put near the fire the heat reflects off the lid onto the cheese and melts it. The inner tray which holds the cheese can then be lifted out for serving. Sometimes the tray is divided into compartments for individual portions. The body can usually be filled with hot water or fitted with a separate plug to keep everything warm.
*The gadroon border on this example echoes those found on salvers of the time.

Silver-mounted bottles
This small late-Victorian silver-mounted glass bottle is typical of the inventiveness of the Victorians. This particular type of object was made as both a vinaigrette – when the sponge is held in a small compartment at the top of the bottle – or alternatively it was produced as a scent bottle. In this case the cork would conveniently hide the necessary glass stopper, and

would be hinged at the neck. These bottles were always looked-after because of their novelty value and consequently most have survived in good condition today.
*Check for chipped glass, a missing stopper or grille, and a dented "cork".

Bleeding bowls
What the British call bleeding bowls are called porringers in the United States (see p.150). They were made in the 17thC and despite their medical name, it is most likely that they were used for food.
This bleeding bowl made in 1699 by Anthony Nelme follows

the standard size and shape. Handles are always pierced, so check carefully for any splits. The bowls should be marked on the rim on the outside – the marks are clearly visible on this example.
*Any bowls which have a mark on the handle as well will command a premium.

Because they were not made in vast quantities they can be expensive – price depends upon the size and weight and the clarity of the marks. The fact that this example has a crest on the handle adds to its value.

DRESS SILVER

A silver belt buckle and belt; Birmingham; 1907; value code E

*A number of decorative dress and dressing table items were made in silver which provide an interesting collecting area today.

Belts

Silver buckles are far more common than silver belts and also more collectable, since belts were so small and few people can fit them round their waists. Buckles are more decorative and are often bought to wear.

The belt in the main picture was made in Birmingham in 1907 and is a fairly typical Edwardian example. Each separate link should be marked – on buckles the two parts should be marked. Demand is high for innovative Art Nouveau designs which demonstrate an individuality in silver which disappeared after c.1940.

Buckles

Silver buckles were made in a wide variety of shapes and sizes, but the more elaborate examples command the highest prices.

This particular buckle is of very high quality and is decorated with an amusing cockatoo design which will immediately increase the price. Both halves of the buckle must be marked with the same marks. Buckles are rarely damaged, although some may be over-polished. This buckle is worth much more than usual because it is cast, which is extremely rare.

Ribbon pullers

Ribbon pullers were possibly used for threading babies' nappies and this is reflected in the design, always the same, of a stork concealing a baby inside its wing. They were made throughout the 19thC but few survive today and as there is little variety prices are usually quite low.

This pair of ribbon pullers is on a stand, but most were free-standing. Quality is generally high and most are still in good condition.
*Ribbon pullers are marked on the inside of the handle.

Dressing table silver

Dressing table silver is far more desirable sold in sets than if sold as individual items. The essential pieces are a hand mirror and hair brushes, but usually far more accessories are included. It is important to check that everything in a set is by the same maker and matches exactly.

Value

Prices vary considerably according to number of pieces in the set, the extent of the decoration and condition. Individual items may be worth very little, but a top of the range set by a prestigious maker such as Levi and Saloman could be worth considerably more.

Less expensive dressing table sets such as the one illustrated below tend to have been used extensively and are frequently quite worn, but more elaborate sets such as the one above were bought primarily for decoration and remain in good condition. Check that the pieces have not been over-polished, causing holes to wear through.
*Some sets have enamelled backs – make sure the enamelling is not chipped.
*Any sets that come in a pretty, fitted box command a premium.

Collecting

Button hooks were made in an infinite variety of sizes and design and have become a serious collecting area among women in particular. Shoe horns are also widely collected. Because they are more practical than button hooks (which cannot be used) they fetch higher prices (around three times as much as a button hook). Shoe horns, particularly smaller examples, are quite easy to damage because their handles are loaded and not very strong.

The type of dressing table silver illustrated below is quite often seen but this set is still very desirable because it is complete, comprising a hand mirror, two hair brushes, a clothes brush (with stiff bristles), a hat brush (with very soft bristles), a comb, shoe horn and button hook. Other sets may include manicure implements. Each item must be marked, but the marks may be quite worn as they are usually close to the edge.

Monograms

Dressing table sets were usually given as presents and should have a mongram or initials engraved on them. The silver is very thin because it is stamped out of sheet and then filled with plaster of Paris and attached to the bristle holder. Consequently it is virtually impossible to remove a crest without leaving the metal impossibly thin. Any that are suspicious should be avoided because there are a lot on the market. Sets with worn brushes should be avoided as it is very expensive to replace the bristles.
*Travelling sets had silver-topped bottles and boxes which must not be chipped or broken. The largest sets have leather blotters and folders.

MISCELLANEOUS

A George III silver cow cremer; John Schuppe; London; 1761; lgth 6in (15.7cm); value code C

*There is a vast range of silverware which cannot be categorized and for which it is impossible to write a checklist. Illustrated below are a number of these items and some useful guides to buying.

Cow creamers

Cow creamers are originally Dutch. They were produced for a very short period between 1755 and 1775 and are rare and collectable today. They were made almost exclusively by the Dutch silversmith John Schuppe, whose mark is hardly ever found on anything else. Most creamers stand on four feet but a few have been fitted with grassy bases. With these it is important to check the base has not been added at a later date to disguise unstable feet.

Cow creamers tend to vary little although some have particularly attractive expressions. The example in the main picture, made by John Schuppe in 1761, has a textured coat, but others may have smooth coats.
*All cow creamers have the fly-hinged cover and tail handle featured here.
* Some cow creamers were made in the 19thC by Charles and George Fox, who are known to have supplied silver to Lambert & Co. Street, London who sold copies of antiques and curios.

Damage

Check that the feet have not cracked and been repaired. As can be seen here, often the back leg has become raised as the jugs were often put down on their back legs first. Check also for cracks at the tail.

German cow creamers

A number of German creamers were made at the beginning of the 20thC. These are significantly larger than English examples and were probably designed to hold milk rather than cream.

Hot milk jugs

Hot milk jugs were made from the beginning of the 18thC when it was fashionable to have hot milk in drinks rather than cream. Most hot milk jugs date from the 1720s. These examples are ovoid in shape and stand on three feet. The earlier style, which is even rarer, is baluster in form and can sometimes also be octagonal. Hot milk jugs tend to be plain apart from engraved arms on a some of the plain baluster-shaped examples.

Honey skeps
Made during the reign of George III these hive-shaped domes were used to hold a glass honey pot. They are usually of very good quality and by fine makers, and although not common a number do appear on the market.

Hot milk jugs were made with either a hinged lid, or a detachable lid as seen on the example illustrated here, which is in the later style.
*Because this hot milk jug dates from 1788 it is likely that it was made to commission, since by this time hot milk jugs had largely been replaced by cream jugs (see pp. 116-119).
*The shield on this jug has been added at a later date and this will considerably reduce the value.
*A surprising number of provincial hot milk jugs were produced in Edinburgh and Newcastle.
*Any jugs made by a particularly desirable maker will command a premium.

This honey skep was made by Paul Storr in 1798 and is worth considerably more than a similar one by a lesser known maker. Skeps tend to be in gilt and have either a crested finial as here, or one in the shape of a bee, which is easier to hold.
*Honey skeps rarely have the glass liner for honey but this makes no difference to the price as it is relatively easy to have a jar made to fit.

Brandy saucepans
Because brandy saucepans vary so much in size it is unlikely than any but the smaller ones were used to heat brandy. They were made in large numbers in a variety of designs, with or without lids. Later pans have hinged lids. They tend to be quite plain, and those which have a band of decoration around the body command the highest prices.

Marks
Brandy saucepans are marked in a group underneath and because they have been subjected to extreme heat many of the marks are now barely visible.
*Any brandy saucepans made by fine makers are particularly desirable.
*Check for any damage, particularly where the handle joins the body.

This brandy saucepan was made in 1725 by George Wickes who produced many similar examples at this time. The plain body on this saucepan is rare as most would have a crest or coat-of-arms.
*Brandy saucepans are relatively abundant and they can be collected quite easily and inexpensively.

NOVELTIES

A mid-19thC children's rattle; value code F

*Some interesting novelty items have been made in silver which are amusing and often inexpensive to collect.

Children's rattles

Children's rattles were made in large numbers and given as christening presents. They are widely available today in a variety of styles. The design in the main picture is by far the most usual and was produced from the second half of the 18thC onwards, in silver, gold and silver gilt. It comprises a whistle, a bell and a piece of coral for the baby to chew on; later 19thC examples had an ivory teething block. The earliest rattles were sometimes made in gold.

Presentation trowels

The quality of presentation trowels varies from plain plated examples with simple handles, to elaborately decorated silver ones with carved ivory handles. They are substantially larger than fish slices – around 10in (23.5cm)

high – and have very sharp blades and are sometimes bought to use as cake slices. If they are of good quality they fetch surprisingly

high prices. Trowels are always inscribed on the back with a record of the event at which they were presented. The arms of the city of London which appear on the example illustrated here add considerably to the price.
*This trowel comes in a fitted case which is very unusual and adds to its desirability.

Inkwells

Novelty inkwells were produced in Germany in the 1900s and imported to Britain, mainly to Birmingham and Chester. They were made especially for the UK market and the quality of the

silver is higher than most German silver (925 instead of 800). They should all bear British hallmarks – if these are missing they are worth substantially less because they would not be allowed to be called silver in Britain. Because these inkwells are amusing items they are popular with collectors and command high prices.
*Sometimes inkwells are surprisingly large – this example is 12in (30cm) long and correspondingly heavy.

Desk accessories

A number of desk items were made in leather fitted with a very fine covering of silver. These are popular as presents today and because they are quite rare they are relatively expensive.

These two items were used to hold blotting paper and stationery. They will both be marked in the piercing and this may be difficult to see, especially if any of the decoration has snapped off. The value of these two items is similar to the rattle.

Care

Any item which has pierced silver mounted onto a leather backing is difficult to clean without staining the surface underneath. The silver is pinned onto the base and it is possible to remove it to clean – however the silver is very flimsy so this should not be done often and it is a good idea to protect it with a spray so that it does not need regular cleaning.

Dressing table mirrors

High-quality silver-framed mirrors are rare and are very keenly sought-after by both private buyers and retail outlets. The borders can be either cast or stamped.

This mirror, made by William Comyns in 1887, is cast and chased and is of far better quality than stamped examples. The largest mirrors tend to command the highest prices – this one is 27in (68cm) high. Very large mirrors are often bought by jewellers for people to use whilst they are trying on their jewelry. Some borders can be more attractive than others. Heart-shaped mirrors are particularly sought after.

Picture frames

Silver picture frames are also highly sought-after because they can be used today. They are smaller than frames made for mirrors and come in a variety of shapes and sizes. Condition of the mount, the velvet backing and the strut are all important. Double frames are popular. Beware modern reproductions where the pattern is very weakly stamped of thin metal.

Cocktail shakers

This electroplated silver "Thirst Extinguisher" is one of a number of similar cocktail shakers made throughout the 1920s. They are popular with collectors because they can still be used. This one has the recipes around the bottom and a strainer spout. Other designs have a window which gives the recipe. When the sleeved barrel is turned to an appropriate arrow the window will give the name of the cocktail. As this type of shaker is more complicated than the one illustrated here it is more expensive. There are many other novelties connected with drink, including bottle holders in the shape of gun carriages.

MARKS OF ORIGIN

London hallmarks

London had an association of goldsmiths in 1180 but it was not legally recognized until 1327 when Edward II passed an Act giving the Worshipful Company of Goldsmiths the right to enforce the assay laws. All London silver of the required quality was marked with the leopard's head, and this became the town mark of London on the introduction of the lion passant in 1544. The marks below are a representative selection of London marks from the reign of Charles II to Victoria.

Charles II (1660)

James II (1685)

William III and Mary II (1689)

William III (1695)

Britannia Standard enforced in 1697
Anne (1702)

George I (1714)

Sterling Standard restored in 1720
George II (1727)

George III (1760)

Duty mark (Sovereign's head) introduced 1784
George IV (1820)

William IV (1830)

Victoria (1837)

Provincial marks

Aside from London a number of the larger towns in Britain had their own assay offices. A selection of marks are featured below.

Birmingham (1773 to present)

Chester (1668-1962)
Marking was not regulated in Chester until the end of the 17thC.

Dublin (1637-present)
From 1637 Dublin's town mark was a crowned harp. In 1731 the figure of Hibernia was added Dublin silver had five marks until 1890 when the duty mark was dropped.

Edinburgh (1552-present)
In 1759 a thistle replaced the assay master's mark and appears on Edinburgh silver until 1975.

Exeter (1701-1882)
In 1701 Exeter's mark changed from "X" to the three-towered castle. The office closed in 1883.

Glasgow (1681-1964)
In 1819 the lion rampant of Scotland and the Sovereign's head were added to the town mark of Glasgow, and in 1914 the thistle standard mark was used.

Norwich (1565-1701)

The city mark changed to a crowned seeded rose in the early 17thC and a stemmed rose at the end of the century.

Sheffield (1773 to present)

York (1559-1856)

The half leopard's head with a fleur-de-lys in a shield was replaced by a half-seeded rose at the end of the 17thC and in 1701 by five lions passant.

Minor Guilds

A number of other towns marked their own silver. A selection of their marks are shown below:

Aberdeen (1600-1880)

Banff (1680-1850)

Bristol (1730-1800)

Canongate (1680-1836)

Cork (1660-1840)

Dundee (1550-1834)

Greenock (1745-1825)

Hull (1570-1710)

Limerick (1710-1800)

Perth (1675-1850)

Taunton (1640-1700)

European city marks

Below are illustrated some of the most common marks of European towns

Amsterdam (Netherlands)

Augsburg (Germany)

Bergen (Norway)

Copenhagen (Denmark)

Hamburg (Germany)

Lisbon (Portugal)

Paris (France)

St Petersburg (Russia)

Turin (Italy)

SELECTED DESIGNERS
& MANUFACTURERS

Hester Bateman (active 1761-1790) Hester Bateman married John Bateman in 1732 and they set up a family business of silversmiths. Although she registered her first mark in 1761, following her husband's death, her mark rarely appears on items made before 1774. From this time onwards she produced a wide range of high-quality silverware, much of which were small domestic items. Her work is usually elegant and attractively engraved.

John Bridge (active 1823-1834)) Went into partnership with Philip Rundell (see below) in c.1788. Together they became goldsmiths and jewelers to King George III in c.1797. Bridge registered two marks in 1823 – the one with a crown featured here is the one most often seen.

John Cafe (active 1740-1757) Registered his first mark in 1740 and his second, more commonly-seen mark in 1742. He monopolized the production of candlesticks, chamber sticks, snuffers and trays in the mid-18thC and his marks are not found on any other kind of silver.

Augustin Courtauld (active 1708-1740s) Apprenticed to Simon Pantin. Registered his first mark (Britannia) in 1708 and subsequent ones in 1729 and 1739. His son, Samuel (b.1720), married Louisa Perina Ogier in 1747 and she registered marks in 1765 as Louisa Courtauld when she had taken over the family business after her husband's death.

Paul Crespin (active 1720-1750s) Much-acclaimed Huguenot silversmith. Registered his first mark in c.1720, and many others – in 1739, 1740 and 1757.

Sebastian and James Crespel (active c.1760-1780s) Well-known 18thC Huguenot makers. Registered their first mark in c.1760. Possibly apprenticed to Edward Wakelin to whom they supplied their silver.

Paul de Lamerie (active 1713-1740s) A Huguenot and the greatest name in English silver. Master of a fluid decorative style. Did not enter a mark until 1733.

Rebecca Emes & Edward Barnard (active 1808-1829) Prolific Regency silversmiths who supplied silver to Rundell, Bridge and Rundell. They registered their first mark together in 1808, and subsequent ones in 1818, 1821 and 1823.

Edward Farrell (active 1813-1840s) A prolific maker during the George IV period of rococo-style silver, particularly known for his teasets decorated with peasant scenes in the style of Teniers.

Charles Fox (active 1822-1840s) Producer of fine-quality domestic silver in an individualistic style. Worked for Lambert & Rawlings of Coventry Street.

Robert Garrard I (active 1792-1800s) and Robert Garrard II (active 1818-1840s) Robert Garrard I went into partnership with John Wakelin from 1792 and was the business descendant of George Wickes. Succeeded by his son Robert Garrard II in 1818, who was later joined by his brothers, James and Sebastian. Became Crown Jewellers in 1843, a position the firm retains today.

Eliza Godfrey (active 1751/2 and 1741-1750s) Married Abraham Buteux and subsequently Benjamin Godfrey. One of the most prolific and sought-after female silversmiths of the 18thC. Produced fine-quality work of Huguenot inspiration, running her husband's business on his death in 1741.

James Gould (active 1722-c.1747) and William Gould (1733-1750) Like the Cafe family the brothers both produced almost exclusively candlesticks in very similar styles in the mid-18thC.

Thomas Hannam & John Crouch (active c.1770-1807) With Crouch Hannam made high-quality salvers and trays in the late 18thC. In partnership with John Crouch II in 1799.

Pierre Harache II (active 1698-1700s) Son of a Huguenot immigrant and one of the greatest makers of the time, following on from his father. Produced restrained and beautifully engraved pieces.

Thomas Heming (active 1745-1780s) Entered his first mark in 1745 and another in c.1767. Appointed jeweler and silversmith to George III in 1760, from which time a crown appeared above his mark until 1782.

Robert Hennell I (active 1763-1811) Producer of good-quality domestic silver. Son of David with whom he registered marks in 1763 and 1768. Also registered marks alone (1772 and 1773) and with his son David (1795) and sons David and Samuel in 1802.

Charles Frederick Kandler (active 1730s-1750s) Important maker of the mid-18thC. Possibly of German origin. Little of his work found today. He registered a mark in partnership with James Murray in 1727, and others on his own in 1739 and 1768.

Anthony Nelme (active 1680-1720s) A native maker who must have had Huguenot immigrants in his workshop. Substantial producer of domestic and display plate. Suceeded by his son Francis who had a very similar Britannia mark.

Simon Pantin (active 1700-1720s) Apprenticed to Pierre Harache. A fine maker of important domestic silver with perhaps not quite as grand a client list as Willaume or his master. Both he and his son of the same name included a peacock in their mark, derived from their address.

Pierre Platel (active 1699-1719) French Huguenot maker of elaborate silver connected with the court. He had many apprentices, amongst whom was the celebrated silversmith Paul de Lamerie.

Benjamin Pyne (active 1680s-1720s) A fine early native maker connected with Hoare's Bank. He produced domestic, civic and ecclesiastical silver. Became Prime Warden of the Goldsmiths' Company in 1725, but died in debt.

Philip Rundell (active 1743-1827) Established the firm of Rundell, Bridge & Rundell (1788-1842), one of London's finest suppliers. In 1788 he joined in partnership with John Bridge and they were joined by Edmund Waller Rundell in 1803. Among the silversmiths working for the firm were Paul Storr, who worked for the firm between 1807 and 1819, and Benjamin Smith.

John Scofield (active 1776-1790s) Maker of superbly crafted elegant silver in restrained late-18thC taste. Probably worked for Jefferys, Jones & Gilbert, Royal Goldsmiths after Thomas Heming.

Benjamin Smith (active 1802-c.1810) Important Regency silversmith supplying a large amount of silver to Rundell, Bridge and Rundell. Similar style to Paul Storr, he specialized in baskets and openwork. With Digby Scott he registered a mark in 1802 and on his own in 1807.

Paul Storr (active 1792-1838) The best-known and most highly-collected silversmith of the early 19thC. He produced silverware for Rundell, Bridge and Rundell between 1807 and 1819. Thereafter Rundell, Bridge and Rundell operated as Storr & Co., and finally as Hunt & Roskill. Storr's mastery of classical and rococo revival themes is unrivalled among British silversmiths.

Edward Wakelin (active 1747-1777) He was in business with George Wickes from 1747 and took over the company in 1758. He went into partnership with the latter's apprentice John Pantin in 1761 until 1777. He was succeeded by his son John, and William Taylor, until 1792 when Taylor was succeeded himself by Garrard. The Wakelins produced good-quality silver throughout their working career.

George Wickes (active 1723-1747) A worthy rival to Paul de Lamerie. He work was influenced by William Kent and the rococo style. He was the maker of much silver for Frederick, Prince of Wales, and a number of other aristocratic patrons.

David Willaume I (active 1690s-1720s) Of French descent. Probably the greatest maker at the beginning of the 18thC, producing silver of the highest quality and supplying to the wealthiest clients in England at this time. He registered marks in c.1697, 1719 and 1720. His son, also called David Willaume (II), was another fine maker of silverware.

GLOSSARY

Alloy A mixture of metals. In the case of silver, the base metals added to strengthen it. Sterling silver is 92.5% pure and is usually mixed with copper.

Applied decoration Decoration added on to the surface of silver, usually cast.

Apostle spoon A spoon with a finial in the shape of one of the Twelve Apostles (*see pp.164-5*). Argyle A silver gravy-warmer with a central well for the gravy and an outer casing for hot water (*see p.144*).

Armorial A full coat-of-arms, but also the term used to describe any item of silver decorated with the owner's coat-of-arms or crest.

Art Deco The style succeeding Art Nouveau (see *below*) in the 1920s developing a linear style in reaction against the curvaciousness of Art Nouveau

Art Nouveau A style defined by its use of dynamic curves based on the shape of flowers, animals, flames and opalescent colours.

Assay The testing of metal to define its purity.

Baize A woollen fabric resembling felt, usually green.

Baluster Architecturally, a short pillar used to support a stair handrail or parapet. In silver, used to define an article with a bulbous body and a long neck.

Baroque A heavy, highly ornamental style which followed classicism in the late 17thC. Used in general for over-ornamented, florid or even grotesque styles.

Bayonet fitting A method of fixing a cover to a body by means of two locking lugs that are slotted into a flange and rotated.

Beading A decorative border of tight beads, usually cast.

Bezel The inner locating rim of a cover on coffee pots, teapots etc, often impressed with marks.

Biggin A small cylindrical coffee or hot water jug with a short spout and domed cover made for a few years in the late 17th and early 18thC.

Bleeding bowl A small shallow dish with two handles used for tasting wine (*see p.173*).

Bright-cut decoration Engraving that causes the decoration to stand out sharply (*see p. 11*).

Bun pepper A pepper caster with a distinctive bulbous body (*see p. 57*).

Cann An American tankard.

Cartouche The decorative frame or panel surrounding a coat-of-arms.

Cast Shaped by pouring molten silver into a cast or mould.

Caudle cup A two-handled drinking cup (*see p.80*).

Chasing Also known as embossing. Decoration worked into the silver with a hammer or punch leaving the pattern raised above the surface.

Chinoiserie The European fashion for decorating silver with naive Oriental figures and scenes fashionable in the late 17thC and again in the mid-18thC.

Close plating The application of a fine layer of silver foil to knives to prevent them from rusting (*see p.137*).

Cut card decoration Flat shapes of applied silver used as decoration and reinforcement, especially around the rims of tea and coffee pots (*see p.12*).

Die stamping A method of production introduced at the end of the 18thC whereby sheet silver is passed between a steel die and drop hammer.

Dish ring Also known as a potato ring (*see p.172*). Used to keep hot dishes away from the table.

Duty dodger An item of silver which has marks taken from another piece in order to avoid paying duty (*see p.10*).

Electroplate Silver applied over a copper or nickel alloy (*see pp142-5*).

Embossing See *chasing*.

Épergne A centrepiece consisting of a central bowl and several smaller bowls that can usually be detached, used from the mid-18thC to display and serve fruit and sweetmeats (*see p. 68*).

Faceted A surface cut into sharp-edged planes in a criss-cross pattern to reflect the light.

Finial The spire-like top on covers for teapots, coffee pots etc. On spoons the ornamental piece at the opposite end of the shaft to the bowl.

Flange A collar or rim applied to an object to strengthen it or for attaching it to another object.

Flat chasing Similar to *chasing*, but with the pattern in low relief.

Flatware A generic term used to describe items of cutlery.

Fluting Close-set concave grooves running vertically up a column or decorative panel.

Freedom box A small commemorative box presented to

prominent citizens when they were given the Freedom of a city in the 18thC and 19thC.

Gadrooning A border composed of a succession of alternating lobes and flutes, usually curved.

Gilding A gold layer applied to a silver or electroplated surface.

Gauge The thickness of a sheet of metal or the diameter of a wire.

Hollow ware Any hollow items such as coffee and tea pots.

Ingot A piece of cast metal obtained from a mould in a form suitable for storage.

Largeworker A maker of large decorative and domestic silver items.

Loading The strengthening and stabilizing of candlesticks by securing an iron rod inside the body using pitch or plaster of Paris.

Liner The inner sleeve of a silver item, made of either silver, plate or glass.

Mantling The background against which a coat-of-arms is displayed.

Matting A non-shiny background for decoration created by either applying acid or punching close-ly-spaced holes onto the surface.

Mirror plateau A flat glass stand upon which is placed a centre piece or épergne to reflect the light (*see p.71*).

Monteith A large shallow bowl with a detachable collar and scalloped rim from which wine glasses were suspended to cool over iced water.

Motte spoon A small spoon with a pierced bowl used to skim tea leaves, with a spike at the end of the stem to unblock the spout of a teapot (*see p.170*).

Moulding Silver decoration cast in a mould.

Nickel A hard white metal similar to silver and equally resistant to oxidation, much used as a substitute for silver in alloys.

Nozzle On a candlestick, the detachable top in which the candle is placed.

Open work Pierced decoration.

Pap boat A small, shallow oval bowl with a lip, used for feeding children or invalids.

Parcel gilt Silver partially covered with gold.

Patina The natural aged surface of silver.

Piercing Intricate cut decoration, originally done with a sharp chis-el, later with a fretsaw, and then punches.

Plinth The square base at the

bottom of a column, for example on candlesticks.

Porringer A two-handled dish, sometimes with a lid, originally used to hold porridge or gruel (*see p.80*).

Pounce A type of talcum powder used to soak up excess ink before the invention of blotting paper.

Regency Literally the period during which George, Prince of Wales, was Prince Regent (1811-1820), but a term used to describe the period from 1800 to William IV. A style characterized by richly-decorated and ornate pieces of silver.

Relief decoration Decoration raised from the surface.

Rococo The extravagant European style which developed out of the Baroque in the mid-18thC, characterized by delicate curvaceous shapes and the use of Chinese and Indian motifs.

Sconce The candle socket of a candlestick. Also, a plate or bracket on the wall to which candle-holders could be attached.

Scroll/flying scroll Curved decoration, particularly used for handles. Flying scroll is an upward scrolling handle which is joined to the body at the base of the scroll only.

Shagreen Untanned leather, originally the skin of the shagri, a Turkish wild ass, but now used to include sharkskin.

Silver gilt Silver covered in a gold layer.

Smallworker Maker of small silver items.

Solder Usually of lead, applied to repair cracks and holes in silver.

Spoonmaker A term used to describe a maker of *flatware*.

Spout cup A covered cup with spout and two handles used for feeding invalids in the early 18thC (*see p.81*).

Swags Decoration of hanging chains of flowers or husks.

Tazza A wide shallow bowl on a stemmed foot.

Trencher An individual small dish for holding salt (*see p.55*).

Tumbler cup A round-bottomed drinking vessel weighted at the base so it will always return to an upright position if upturned.

Vesta box An ornate case for carrying matches (*see p.163*).

Vinaigrette A small silver box with an inner pierced lid to hold a sponge soaked in a vinegar, an early version of smelling salt.

Waiter A small salver, less than 6in (15cm) in diameter.

INDEX

ACKNOWLEDGMENTS

The publishers would like to thank the following auction houses, museums, dealers, collectors and other sources for supplying pictures for use in the book

p.1 SL; **p.3** SL; **p.11**t CL, c SL, b SL; **p.12**l SL, r SL; **p.13** SL; **p.14** SL, **p.15** SL; **p.16**IB/MB**p.18** IB/MB; **p.19** lSL, r IB/MB; **p.20** tl IB/MB, bl IB/MB, r IB/MB; **p.21** l SL, r IB/MB; **p.22** IB/MB, **p.23**l SL, r SL; **p.24**l CNY, tr CNY, br SL; **p.25**tr SL, b SL; **p.26** SL; **p.27** tl SNY, bl IB/MB, tr SL, br SL; **p.28** CNY; **p. 29**l SL, tr SL, br SL; **p.32** IB/MB **p.34** CNY; **p.35**l CNY, tr SL, br SL; **p.36** CSc, **p.37**tl SL, bl SL, tr SL, br SL; **p.38**t IB/MB, b IB/MB; **p.39** tl IB/MB, tr SL, b SL; **p.40** IB/MB; **p.41**t CNY, l IB/MB, r IB/MB; **p.42** IB/MB; **p.43**tl CNY, cl IB/MB, b SL; **p.44** SL; **p.45**tl SL, cl SL, b SL, tr IB/MB; **p.46** IB/MB; **p.47**t SNY, bl CL, br CNY; **p.48**t SL, bl CNY, br SL; **p.49** tl CNY, tr SL, b CNY; **p.50** CNY; **p.51**tl SL, tr CNY, b IB/MB; **p.52** IB/MB; **p.53**tl SL, bl SL, r IB/MB; **p.54** SL; **p.55**tl CNY, cl SNY, bl IB/MB, tr IB/MB, br IB/MB; **p. 56** IB/MB; **p. 57**tl IB/MB, bl IB/MB, tr IB/MB, br IB/MB; **p.58** IB/MB; **p.59**cl IB/MB, bl IB/MB, tr JW, br IB/MB; **p.60** Cl; **p.61**tlSNY, bl CL, r CL; **p.62**CNY; **p.66**SL**p.63**tSL, cCNY, b SL; **p.68** SNY; **p.69**tl SL, c SNY, b SL; **p.70** CL, **p.71**l SL, tr SL, SL; **p.72** SNY; **p.73**t SNY, c SL, b DN; **p.74**t SL, b SL; **p.75**cl SSc; tr SL, b SL; **p.76** SL; **p.77**tl SL, cl SL, r CNY, b SL; **p.78** CNY; **p.79**t SL, bl CL, cr CL; **p.80**t IB/MB, b SL; **p. 81**tl SL, tr SL, bSL; **p.82** IB/MB; **p.84** SNY, **p.85**tl SNY, bl IB/MB, tr CNY, br SL, **p.86** IB/MB; **p.87**l SL, tr SL, br IB/MB; **p. 89**tl IB/MB, bl IB/MB, r IB/MB; **p.90** SL; **p.91**tl SL/IB, tr SL, bl SL, br SL; **p.92** SL; **p.93**tl SL, bl SL, r SL; **p.94** SL; **p.95**tl SL, tr CNY, b IB/MB; **p.96** IB/MB; **p.98** SL; **p.99**t SL, bl SL, br SL; **p.100**t IB/MB, bsL; **p.101**t SL, cr SL, b SNY; **p.102** SL; **p.103**tl SNY, tr IB/MB, b SNY; **p.104**t IB/MB; b IB/MB; **p.105**cl SL, tr SL, b SL; **p.106** SL; **p.107**t SL, c SL, b SL; **p.108**t SL; **p.109**tl SNY, tr CNY, b SL; **p.110**t SL, bl IB/MB, br IB/MB; **p.111**tl SL, cr SL, bSL; **p.112** IB/MB; **p.113**tl SL, cl SL, b CNY, r SL; **p.114** IB/MB; **p.115** SL, bl SL, r SL; **p.116** SL; **p.117**tl SL, bl CNY, tr SNY, br IB/MB; **p.118**t IB/MB; b SL; **p.119**tl SNY, tr SNY, b SL; **p.124** IB/MB; **p.126** IB/MB, **p.127**l SL, r SL; **p.128**t IB/MB, b IB/MB; **p.129**l SL, tr SL, br SL; **p.130** IB/MB; **p.131**tl IB/MB, tr SL, b SL; **p.132/3** SL; **p.134** SNY; **p.135**tl SL, tr SNY, b SL; **p.136** SL; **p.138** IB/MB; **p.139**tl IB/MB, bl IB/MB, tr CNY, br CNY; **p.140**t SL, bl IB/MB, br SL; **p.141** IB/MB; **p.142** SL; **p.143**t SL, b JW; **p.144**tl JW, bl IB/MB, r IB/MB; **p.145**tl SL, tr SL, b SL; **p.146** SNY; **p.148** CNY; **p.149**tl SNY, cl CNY, b CNY, r CNY; **p.150**tl CNY, tr CNY, b SNY; **p.151**t SNY, cl CNY, cr SNY, br SNY; **p.152** SNY; **p.153** SNY; **p.154**t CNY, bl SNY, br SNY; **p.155**t CNY, c SNY, b SNY; **p.156** SL; **p.158** IB/MB; **p.159**t SL, bl IB/MB, cr SL; **p.160**t SL, b SL; **p.161**tl CEd, cl CEd, bl CNY, tr CNY, br SL; **p.162**l SL, r SL; **p.163** cl SL, tr SL, cr SL, b SL; **p.164/5** SL; **p.166**t IB/MB, b IB/MB; **p.167** tl SL, tr SL, b SL; **p.168** SL; **p.169**t CNY, c IB/MB, b IB/MB; **p.170**tl SL, tr SL, b SL; **p.171**l Tess., r CNY; **p.172**t IB/MB, b IB/MB; **p.173**tl SL, tr SL, b SL; **p.174**t IB/MB, bl SL, br SL; **p.175**t SL, b SL; **p.176** MB; **p.177**tl SL, tr SL, b SL; **p.178**SL; **p.179**t SL, bl SL, r IB/MB.

KEY
b bottom, c centre , l left, r right

CEd	Christies Edinburgh		taken by Ian Booth
CL	Christies London		for Mitchell Beazley
CNY	Christies New York		at Sotheby's
Csc	Christies Scotland	JW	John Wilson
DN	Dreweatt Neate	SL	Sotheby's London
IB/MB	Specially commis-	SNY	Sotheby's New York
	sioned photographs	Tess.	Tessiers

Special thanks to Sotheby's London silver department for their help in finding many of the pictures for this book.

BIBLIOGRAPHY

Assay Offices of Great Britain
  *Hallmarks on Gold Silver &
  Platinum*
Banister, Judith, *English Silver
  Hallmarks*, Foulsham and Co.
  Ltd, 1970
Bly, John, *Discovering Hallmarks
  on English Silver*, Shire
  Publications Ltd., 1968
Bly, John, *Silver and Sheffield Plate
  Marks*, Mitchell Beazley, 1993
Bradbury, Frederick, *Bradbury's
  Book of Hallmarks*, J. W.
  Northend Ltd., 1988
Brett, Vanessa, *The Sotheby's
  Directory of Silver*, Sotheby's,
  1986
Culme, John, *The Directory of Gold
  and Silversmiths, Jewellers and
  Allied Traders 1838-1914*,
  Antique Collector's Club
Feild, Rachael, *Buying Antique
  Silver and Sheffield Plate*,
  Macdonald Orbis, 1988
Grimwade, Arthur G., *London
  Goldsmiths 1697-1837 Their
  Marks and Lives*, Faber and
  Faber, 1976
Hughes, Therle, *The Country Life
  Antiques Handbook*, Country
  Life Books, 1986

Jackson, Sir Charles J., *English
  Goldsmiths and Their Marks*,
  Dover Publications Inc, 1921
Knowles, Eric, *Miller's Antiques
  Checklist: Victoriana*, Mitchell
  Beazley, 1991
Knowles, Eric, *Miller's Antiques
  Checklist: Art Nouveau*, Mitchell
  Beazley, 1992
Kovel, Ralph M. and Terry H.,
  *American Silver, Pewter and
  Silver Plate*, Crown Publishers,
  1961
Miller, Judith and Martin,
  Understanding Antiques, Mitchell
  Beazley, 1989
Miller, Judith and Martin, eds,
  *Miller's Pocket Dictionary of
  Antiques*, Mitchell Beazley, 1990
Savage, George, *Dictionary of
  Antiques*, 2nd edition, Barrie and
  Jenkins, 1978
Tardy, *International Hallmarks on
  Silver*, Tardy, 1985
Waldron, Peter, *The Price Guide to
  Antique Silver*, Antique
  Collector's Club, 1982
Ward, Susan, *Catalogue of
  American Antiques*, Apple Press
  Ltd., 1990